LEAD for GOOD

FIELD GUIDE

7 Steps for Unleashing the Great Nonprofit Leader Within

Karen Ramsey

LEAD for GOOD

This publication has been developed to benefit nonprofit and other social sector organizations. Therefore, the purchaser of this work is granted limited permission to reproduce the tools herein. This includes worksheets, forms, charts, graphics, and brief excerpts so long as the reproductions are attributed to Lead for Good and are for direct use by the individual or organization that purchased the *Field Guide*. Permission to copy is not granted to individuals outside of the purchasing organization.

Tools and text MAY NOT be reproduced for training outside of the purchasing organization. For example, a consultant may not purchase one copy of this work and then use the tools with multiple organizations. In this case, an organization that a consultant is working with should purchase a copy of the *Field Guide*, and then may distribute copied tools to members of the purchasing organization.

Umbrella organizations may not purchase a single copy of the *Field Guide* and make copies of tools for member organizations under its umbrella. Volume discounts are available. Please contact Lead for Good at www.LeadforGood.org to make arrangements.

ISBN 978-1-628-906-34-9 - Paperback
ISBN 978-1-943-090-66-2 - eBook

Cover and book design by Amanda Graff
www.dreamgraffx.com

DEDICATION

This *Field Guide* is dedicated to
Leslie Moore and Paul Elliott.
Thank you both for making it a reality.
I wouldn't have gotten it done without you.

CONTENTS

CONTENTS

CONTENTS

CONTENTS

GET TOOLS

All of the blank tools in the *Field Guide* are available for download. To access the tools online, registration is required at www.LeadforGood.org.

Once you register, you will receive an email confirmation. The following password must be entered to access the tools: **FG_tools**.

ACKNOWLEDGEMENTS

Creating this *Field Guide* has been a journey and there are many people who have helped along the way. From the very beginning, when I jumped out of bed in the middle of the night to jot down the initial outline, my husband, Rick Ramsey, has been a steadfast supporter.

Others provided support either by contributing to the content and/or providing feedback on the final product. My heartfelt thanks goes to these individuals. Some of those who helped include:

Laura Atwood
Debra Bradley
Michael Darcy
Debra Exner
Elaine Fogel
Amanda Graff
Maddie Hunter
Julie Iacobelli
Karen Ailsworth Kinzer
Mike Nolan
Cassandra O'Neill
Gayle Pincus
Stephanie Small
Susan Kenny Stevens
Elana Sullivan
Linda Volhein
Audrey Wyatt
Alan Young

FORWARD

> Leadership. A loaded concept if there ever was one.
>
> **Susan Kenny Stevens, Ph.D.**

By Susan Kenny Stevens, Ph.D.
Author *Nonprofit Lifecycles*

I've spent my entire career working in and for the nonprofit sector first as a clinical social worker and later as a strategic consultant and advisor to hundreds of foundations, social service and arts organizations. Had you asked me to define "leadership" at the beginning of my career, my definition would certainly have been a lofty, yet unrealistic and unachievable one. And, it continues to morph.

Whether you are a seasoned nonprofit executive, board member or manager, or you are new to one of these tasks, Karen Ramsey's *Lead for Good Field Guide: Seven Steps for Unleashing the Great Nonprofit Leader Within* provides seminal leadership strategies that are solid, practical and user-friendly. Most importantly, they are doable, because that's who leaders are. They do good things that move their organizations forward.

Leaders are people to look up to. I once thought of leadership as something grand. Leaders certainly weren't ordinary people, they were superheroes. Then I began my consulting business. There I got a panoramic view of the true leadership taking place each and every day in the nonprofit sector. Rather than some unattainable goal accomplished only by the chosen few, I witnessed dozens of nonprofit executives, staff and board members bravely tackle important tasks to move their organizations and missions forward.

These were not superheroes. They were ordinary folks stepping up to difficult challenges and creative opportunities, often without any prior background in meeting these types of challenges.

It was then I realized that leadership comes in several sizes and shapes. It's not a one-size-fits-all phenomenon. You're not born with it. It's not something you earn by wealth or privilege or the school you attended. And above all, it's not just for superheroes.

Instead, leadership occurs when ordinary nonprofit executives, board and staff members take on the important tasks that lead to organizational progress and success.

Daily leadership opportunities will continue as long as there are nonprofit organizations filling society's social and cultural gaps. Few of us will ever gain superhero status in our fields. But if we stay in the nonprofit sector long enough, we will all face numerous stepping-up opportunities. And for those moments, aren't we lucky to have Karen Ramsey's *Lead for Good* as our field guide!

WHY THIS FIELD GUIDE

Here's the story behind the *Field Guide*: For years I worked as vice president of human resources for a Fortune 500 company. Part of my training involved participating in an executive development program. Through it and years of experience, I amassed an arsenal of tools that strengthened my leadership skills.

Any time I got the chance, I worked as a volunteer in the nonprofit sector. Once I began serving on various boards of directors for the causes I championed, it became clear that many of the nonprofit leaders had not had the same leadership learning opportunities I'd had as a private sector executive. I became convinced that if nonprofit leaders had access to the same tools as the ones I had honed, they would become more effective, make better use of limited resources, and their organizations would thrive. The *Field Guide* is my effort to bring those tried-and-true resources to you.

> The quality of leadership, more than any other single factor, determines the success or failure of an organization.
>
> **Fred Fiedler and Martin Chemers**

In 2001, I left the private sector to dedicate myself full-time to helping social sector leaders become stronger. I realized that supporting people doing work for social good was far more satisfying to me than supporting people who were focused on increasing their company's bottom line. While leaders expressed a desire to learn and grow, they confided that they were embarrassed they didn't already possess the skills, and that they struggled to justify to their boards of directors the cost of investing in their personal development.

I figured out a way to fill the gap between what nonprofit leaders needed and what they said they could afford. The answer lay in finding and partnering with corporations and other funders to underwrite the cost to make leadership development attainable. And so began the launch of my own nonprofit organization, Lead for Good. This was in 2008, and the economy was in the throes of a major downturn. Nonprofits experienced drastic funding cuts just as the demand for their services was on the rise. Lead for Good was incorporated as a nonprofit dedicated to the fundamental proposition: "Every nonprofit organization thrives with great leadership."

In hindsight, that was not the perfect time for me to get started, but I jumped in with both feet buoyed by passion, energy, and optimism. A little more than one year later, as my board of directors was settling in and we were going through the complicated and daunting process of becoming a 501 (c)3, I was diagnosed with a rare genetic disorder called von Hippel-Lindau Syndrome, meaning I am predisposed to both benign and cancerous tumors. My projected life expectancy indicated that I should have already been dead. Welcomed recalculations combined with ongoing surgeries to remove cancerous tumors have given me strength to move forward on my chosen career path.

Recuperating also gives me the luxury of uninterrupted think time to plan and further support Lead for Good. Publishing this *Field Guide* within the context of my own story is one positive tangible gleaned from an otherwise gloomy prognosis.

The *Field Guide* is designed to serve as a concise and well-signposted pathway regarding seven steps you can take to make a transition from being a good leader to becoming a great leader in the nonprofit sector. The *Guide* is based on my expertise while drawing richly on the experiences and wisdom of great leaders I know and trust.

Threaded through the *Field Guide* are three important themes. The first is that truly great leaders make time to reflect creatively and wisely on their activities. They strive to avoid burnout by establishing a balance between enjoying life and doing right by their organizations. The second theme is that leading an organization is a team activity, not an endeavor to be attempted alone. Acknowledging that one can't be perfect at everything and drawing on the expertise of others is critically important. Support and guidance can come from within the organization or from external resources available through volunteers or for hire. And, the final theme is that truly great leaders empower others and work hard to ensure they are succeeded by people with the same values and skills. The *Field Guide* is intended to help top executives encourage those with talent to enthusiastically step into executive director positions as they become available. It is also intended to provide ideas and tools to anyone interested in honing his or her leadership skills in the nonprofit sector, whether or not he or she chooses to step into a senior leadership position.

As you use this *Field Guide,* please keep in mind that it is unrealistic to implement everything at once. It is not reasonable to expect to flawlessly integrate all seven competencies. Mistakes should be viewed as learning opportunities. Remember to tap into the strengths of others to prevent working in a vacuum. Inviting help is a sign of strength, not weakness. Whether it's tapping into the expertise of someone involved with your organization or hiring an outside professional, getting support is a smart move.

My hope is that you will discover that you can create a lasting legacy while "having it all." Implementing the seven competencies and using the tools provided will help you create a balanced and rewarding personal life, a successful and sustainable organization, and a culture that is focused on developing the next generation of great nonprofit leaders.

Go forth and lead,

Karen Ramsey

HOW TO USE THIS FIELD GUIDE

If you're reading this, you have made the decision to pursue leadership in the nonprofit sector. The *Field Guide* outlines seven key steps and provides **47** work tools that individually and collectively help a nonprofit executive successfully lead his/her organization. Each chapter covers one of the seven core competencies, or steps, that promise to make you a stronger leader. Information includes illustrative narrative and specific tools that are helpful in supporting each competency. The *Guide* provides an overview of each of the steps and is designed as a ready reference to be accessed as issues arise.

In many cases, completed examples of the tools appear in the Tools Section at the end of each chapter. For a list of the tools as they appear in each chapter, refer to the Table of Contents.

Ready to use versions of each tool are available at the end of the *Field Guide*. Tools are listed alphabetically on page 135.

Once you have purchased a copy of the *Field Guide* and registered on the Lead for Good website, downloadable versions of each tool are available for your use. Go to www.LeadforGood.org. The following password must be entered to access the tools: **FG_tools**.

Throughout the *Field Guide* you will notice the use of such terms as "executive director," "chief executive," "CEO," "ED," and "leader." Each of these is intended to be synonymous and are used in this manuscript interchangeably. In addition, while the primary focus is on those who run nonprofits, the advice and tools are applicable to employees at all levels, board members, and those working in any social sector organization.

There is no requirement to work your way through the seven steps in order. Instead, thumb through the pages and prioritize areas you want to tackle. This way you are not

THE 7 STEPS

STEP 1

Know Your Mission and Purpose

STEP 2

Invest in Self and Others

STEP 3

Think Strategically

STEP 4

Inspire Others

STEP 5

Share Leadership

STEP 6

Build Strong Community Relationships

STEP 7

Achieve Results

overwhelmed by the volume of tools at your disposal or confused by myriad directions you can go.

As you scan the material, you are likely to identify areas where you are already a strong leader and areas you haven't yet experienced. To establish momentum, begin by picking one of those strong areas and use the tools to leverage your strength to its fullest potential. At the same time, tackle a leadership area or two you haven't yet explored. Select those you believe are realistic and achievable within the next 12 months. Use the personal development planning tool included in Chapter One of the *Field Guide* to create a written roadmap that outlines the steps you intend to take. Let others, including your boss or board chair, know what you are working on and ask for feedback as you experiment and make changes. Determine whether the actions you are taking are having a positive impact and make adjustments as necessary.

Once you begin executing your plan and experimenting with the tools, you will measurably improve the quality of your leadership.

As we know, the long-term success of an organization depends on the strength of its leadership. So, the investment you are making now in yourself will generate exponential dividends for both you and your organization in the future.

CHAPTER ONE ● STEP 1
KNOW YOUR MISSION AND PURPOSE

Strong, successful leaders know themselves and keep a clear vision of their end goals. They follow their passions and choose work based on them. They capitalize on their strengths and abilities while striving to shore up areas where they have admitted gaps. They know where to find and when to find support they need.

Leading a nonprofit organization is extremely hard work that is not well compensated. Few enter the nonprofit sector looking for wealth, 9-to-5 working hours, or sumptuous environments. Most people follow their passion to give back to others and make a difference in their communities.

> The very essence of leadership is that you have to have vision.
>
> Theodore Hesburgh

The most successful nonprofit leaders start or join organizations based on their desires to support a specific mission. They either have personal experience with the cause, or their hearts and minds have been touched in telling ways, as happened to Linda Volhein.

Revealing Your Passion

What is your passion? What is the personal driving force on which you want to capitalize? Perhaps you already know, as many do from the outset—and as we see reflected in so many personal narratives, biographies, and obituaries. Others might not know or might still be pondering alternatives. If you're unsure, I recommend you try using the simple, excellent tool called Appreciative Interview/ Peak Experience Exercise. A blank template of the Appreciative Interview/ Peak Experience Exercise can be found on page 138.

For a downloadable version go to www.LeadforGood.org.

The concept of appreciative interview was first introduced by David Cooperrider. This approach will help you to identify what brings you joy, and in what direction you should focus your energy. It will also help you to identify strengths and abilities you bring to the world. Don't be surprised by the direction the exercise might take you. When I first completed it many years ago, while still working in the private sector, I realized then that my passion lay in working in the nonprofit sector. As a human resources executive I was only partially satisfied. I could help people learn, grow and achieve their dreams, but it didn't make my heart sing the way it did when I was performing community service in support of an inner-city program working with at-risk youth. It was at that point that I began the ground work to move into the nonprofit sector.

Defining Your Personal Vision/Purpose

Another tool you might find helpful in unlocking your own personal passion is the Personal Vision Statement Exercise. Once you complete the exercise, reflect on your answers in order to create a concise personal vision statement. The vision statement should identify the end game you want to accomplish. It should reflect

THE PASSION AND MISSION OF LINDA VOLHEIN

As CEO of Florence Crittenton in Phoenix, Arizona, from 1993 to 2011, Linda Volhein devoted herself to providing pregnant teenagers with safe haven and services. Her mission and that of the organization were the same: "Give every girl whose life we touch safety, hope and opportunity."

During her 18-year tenure, Linda's unwavering vision, tenacity and passion to her cause led to an evolution of the Florence Crittenton facility. Under her leadership, it grew from a dilapidated, 7,000-square-foot building designed to serve 20 delinquent girls to a 45,000-square-foot campus that includes a junior high charter school. The Florence Crittenton campus now annually serves more than 2,000 young women and their families.

Linda's decision to join Florence Crittenton as a caseworker just out of college had stemmed from her own history as a teenage mother. From a devout Catholic family, her parents commanded her to drop out of high school at 15 and marry the father of her unborn child. The marriage failed and so did young Linda's attempt to go back to high school. Students shunned her while school administrators shamed her. She left after a day and a half.

Stinging from her experience and feeling ill equipped as a young mother, she decided that she would dedicate her life to helping other young women who were abandoned by their families and communities by their circumstances or choices. Fueled by passion, she finally earned her GED at the age of 22, and then continued to college where she earned a degree in social work.

your long-term goal and the legacy you hope to leave. I'll use myself as an example. My personal vision is "Every nonprofit leader I touch becomes a better leader." I work to make the touch happen through a variety of outreach efforts, including this *Field Guide*, the development of Lead for Good's Executive Director and Leader Succession Institutes, and meaningful coaching conversations I have with leaders. A blank template of the Personal Vision Statement Exercise can be found on page 192. For a downloadable version go to www.LeadforGood.org.

Identifying Your Overall Strengths

Great nonprofit leaders manage to combine their passions with their overall abilities and strengths. I encourage you to explore what attributes you have to contribute to moving your career and organization forward. In the nonprofit leadership course I taught at Arizona State University (ASU), students completed the instrument found in the book *Strengths Based Leadership* by Tom Rath and Barry Conchie.[1] Using a unique code found in each copy of the book, a report generated after taking a brief on-line survey outlines an individual's top five of 34 Clifton StrengthsFinder themes, and shares personalized strengths insights. These insights fall under four domains of leadership strength, which are all clearly defined in the book. The four domains include executing, influencing, relationship building, and strategic thinking. Knowing your top strengths and dominant domain of leadership helps you clarify how you can leverage those strengths to enhance your satisfaction at work and best support your nonprofit organization. A former student recently told me that she talked about the strengths identified by the instrument as she was interviewing for a new position. She believes clarity gleaned from the tool was a pivotal component in helping her land the job!

Here's another example of how the instrument works. A colleague of mine, a nonprofit executive director, shares the results of her survey. Her top five Clifton StrengthsFinder themes are: Strategic, Ideation, Relator, Input and Individualization. The following provides brief definitions included in her report to give you a sense of what each theme means in the context of her other strengths. It gives you a flavor of the type of information contained in the assessment report.

> **Strategic** - She feels satisfied with life when her innovative thinking style is appreciated. She automatically identifies trends, sees problems, and pinpoints opportunities not seen by others.

Ideation – She is creative and great at brainstorming ideas. She is imaginative and has the assertiveness to speak up and share her thoughts.

Relator – She tends to have the ability to distill a complex or layered idea into its essence so that others are able to better understand it. She is also drawn to learning and gaining knowledge and skills and tends to bond with those who are able to articulate what they want to achieve in life.

Input – By nature, she is constantly on the lookout for new ideas and knowledge. She is a voracious reader and is driven to have an impact and push for change that benefits humanity.

Individualization – She is able to sense the feelings and perspectives of others. It is very satisfying when she is able to figure out why someone reacts or behaves differently than she, and she delights in helping others gain knowledge and skill.

As for how her themes fit into the leadership domain strengths, according to Rath and Conchie three of the five (Strategic, Ideation and Input) fall under the domain of Strategic Thinking. "Leaders with great Strategic Thinking strengths are the ones who keep us all focused on what could be. They are constantly absorbing and analyzing information and helping the team make better decisions. People with strengths in this domain continually stretch our thinking for the future."[2]

Identifying Your Leadership Strengths and Opportunities from a 360 Perspective

Once you've clearly identified your passions and your overall strengths, the next step is to solicit feedback from others regarding the effectiveness of your leadership. It is extremely helpful to understand how others perceive the way you lead. If you don't know what others are thinking about your efforts, how will you ever grow and develop? Great leaders are not static; they use information from others to make necessary adjustments.

Among essential tools available for exploring this critical subject is a proven, wide-angle methodology known as the 360-degree assessment (the 360). It's designed as a template to gauge what successful leaders do, and aspire to do, and allows key constituents to rate how well an individual is delivering on those specific leadership attributes. Constituent feedback re-enforces things a leader is doing right, and allows for tweaking areas that are not perceived by others to be as strong. Feedback is a good thing, not to be confused with a "bad rating" or exposing a weak spot. All great leaders need feedback to stay great and continue to grow.

Lead for Good has developed a proprietary nonprofit leadership 360. It provides a vehicle for others to rate an individual on her or his leadership performance. The Lead for Good version measures attributes that support each of the seven leadership steps, or the seven competencies, found in this *Field Guide*. To use it, chief executives take the instrument themselves and invite their board chairs, board members, staff members, and key volunteers to complete it. If the organization is small, it may also be appropriate to ask program or service recipients to complete the assessment. An additional version of the 360 instrument is also available for ready-next leaders who are poised to step into more responsible leadership roles. For more information go to www.LeadforGood.org.

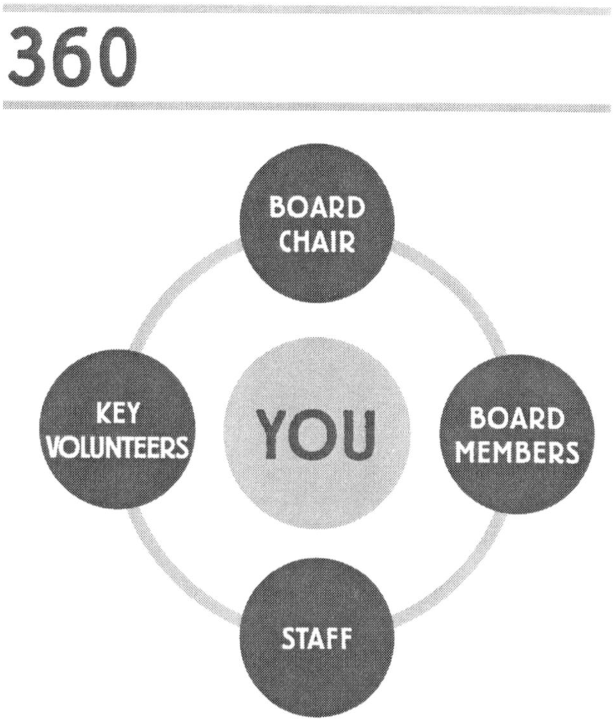

Getting SMART and Making Your Own Personal 360-Based Development Plan

After taking the 360, create a development plan. A completed example of a Personal Development Plan can be found in the Tools Section at the end of this chapter. For a blank template go to page 191. For a downloadable version go to www.LeadforGood.org.

Your plan will need to describe what you intend to do to enhance your leadership effectiveness, how you plan to accomplish it, and offer a schedule for making it happen. Don't try to tackle all seven competencies at once. Pick one area in which your scores were high, and select one or two areas where you'd like to improve your scores. Your plan should be SMART—that is, written with **S**pecific, **M**easurable, **A**chievable, **R**ealistic, and **T**ime-sensitive results. The strongest plans identify specific competencies/objectives and list two or more action steps under each that you intend to take to make progress toward your goals. Be realistic about getting support to develop the plan. Consult others, such as an experienced colleague, coach or adviser, for help completing it and assessing its practicality.

Choosing Your Mission

Once you have revealed your passion, strengths, and personal vision and have established clarity around your plans for growth and development, the next critical step is to make sure there is alignment between your vision and the stated mission of your organization. If you are an Executive Director, you have a modicum of control over the direction of the organization.

However, it remains the purview of the board of directors to set the vision and mission. As a result, you might find yourself in a position that is no longer a good fit for you. In that case, you have choices: 1) have a conversation with the board chair to explore the potential of shifting the organization's mission; or 2) begin looking for a position somewhere else. A third option, which I do not recommend, is to tough it out and see what the future brings to your organization. Your personal vision will serve as a trusted guide in your decision-making.

In light of changes afoot in the nonprofit sector, you might be hesitant to plunge back into the job market. Recent studies indicate many nonprofit leaders are planning to retire over the next five years, however, so start looking now for opportunities to move to a job that better suits you. With clarity about your personal vision, you have a stronger likelihood of landing a job in an organization that is aligned with your purpose. During the selection process, your energy and enthusiasm will come through loud and clear. Do not leave your current position until you've secured a new one. In general, it's much easier to find a job when you already have a job.

The Take Away

If you are using this *Field Guide*, you are either currently working in, or considering a shift to, the nonprofit sector. If you are a veteran and intend to continue this path or are just beginning the journey, be clear on who you are, what you intend to contribute, and how you want to be in the world. Align your passion with the work you do every day and the quality of your life will be greatly enhanced. Some studies show this balance might even prolong your life. Doing satisfying work feels good. Go for it!

TOOLS ● STEP 1

KNOW YOUR MISSION AND PURPOSE

EXAMPLE

PERSONAL DEVELOPMENT PLAN

	RESULTS EXPECTED (Measure Of Success)	TARGET DATE	ASSISTANCE REQUIRED	BUDGET CONSIDERATIONS
Key Competency: **INVEST IN SELF AND OTHERS**	Maintain overall 360 feedback score on this competency at 80 percent favorable or better	Follow-Up 360 assessment to be conducted in 12 months	Same participants who completed the recent assessment	Cost to purchase assessment
Action 1: Keep budget dollars for training and development for staff as part of the upcoming budgeting cycle	$500 available to support staff to attend mutually agreed upon learning opportunities	Include in annual budget and an appropriate amount each year thereafter	Board	$500
Action 2: Commit to being home even more with my family	Be home by 6 pm three days per week	Begin NOW	None	No Cost
Action 3: Build board development opportunities into meetings in addition to the annual board retreat	Include 30-minute learning sessions in four board meetings per year	Begin within 6 months	Board Chair	Cost to join BoardSource.org to get ideas on board development topics

PERSONAL DEVELOPMENT PLAN - Page 2

	RESULTS EXPECTED (Measure Of Success)	TARGET DATE	ASSISTANCE REQUIRED	BUDGET CONSIDERATIONS
Key Competency: **SHARE LEADERSHIP**	Improve overall 360 feedback score on this competency by at least 5 percentage points from 70 percent favorable to 75 percent favorable	Follow up 360 assessment to be conducted in 12 months	Same participants who completed recent assessment	Cost to purchase assessment
Action 1: Set up bi-weekly meetings with each direct report to discuss activities, clarify level of authority for each activity, identify where support is needed and check in on progress for each commitment	Those who report to me indicate on the assessment that they clearly understand expectations	Schedule in place within three months	Staff that reports directly to me	No Cost
Action 2: Place agreed-upon due dates for all major projects, including staff, board, volunteer and collaborations into my outlook calendar with a reminder message two weeks in advance	Follow up with staff 95 percent of the time on project deadlines	Begin using this process no later than 30 days from now	None	No Cost
Action 3: Meet one-on-one with board chair to track progress, keep her informed and offer support as needed	Meet with board chair four times during fiscal year	Meet quarterly beginning at the start of the fiscal year	Board Chair	No Cost

PERSONAL DEVELOPMENT PLAN - Page 3

	RESULTS EXPECTED (Measure Of Success)	TARGET DATE	ASSISTANCE REQUIRED	BUDGET CONSIDERATIONS
Key Competency: **ACHIEVE RESULTS**	Complete 95 percent of commitments	Review commitment completion rate in 12 months	None	No Cost
Action 1: Proactively set due dates for projects I am responsible for executing in the strategic plan	100 percent of deadlines determined for delivery in fiscal year	Begin negotiating due dates 60 days prior to start of fiscal year	None	No Cost
Action 2: Place all deadlines in Microsoft Outlook with a two-week reminder prior to due date to include new commitments as they arise, even if they are small	100 percent of all deadlines entered into Outlook	All commitments are put in calendar with reminder beginning in the new fiscal year	None	No Cost
Action 3: Buy flowers for myself every time I meet or beat a deadline	Buy flowers every time I successfully meet a deadline	Purchase flowers within one week of accomplishment of deadline	None	$15 per bouquet

CHAPTER TWO ● STEP 2
INVEST IN SELF AND OTHERS

Effective leaders invest in themselves, their employees and their boards. They know the value of this investment even in light of forced budget cutting and belt tightening. Even in good times, some nonprofit CEO's believe dollars spent on improving skills is money diverted from the mission. My research indicates that spending money to support CEO development and the growth of employees and board members is one of the best investments an organization can make.

> "Leadership and learning are indispensable to each other."
>
> John F. Kennedy

While it is sometimes difficult to quantify the exact impact of skill development, results include process improvement, productivity gains, and higher job satisfaction (which translates to lower employee turnover.) Christine Odom, a nonprofit CEO client, experienced a $100,000 net increase in revenue as a result of investing time and money in her personal development. That was just in the first year! Her introspection and hard work to understand her leadership strengths and improve on weaknesses led to a promotion at the organization's national headquarters. "Once we better understood how to work as a team, we valued and appreciated our differences much more. And, I got better at delegation and made progress on how I managed myself when stressful situations arose," says Odom.

Failure to recognize and invest in supporting your needs and those of other key stakeholders in your organization leads to job dissatisfaction, burnout, and, ultimately expensive turnover.

Calculating the Cost of Failing to Invest in Yourself and Employees

In my 13 years as a human resource executive at a Fortune 500 company, I witnessed the hidden costs associated with neglecting staff needs. By demonstrating the costs associated with turnover, and inversely, the potential savings by retaining staff, I made a successful business case. The company changed its culture to invest in employee development and raise salaries. Over time, this strategy saved the company money which allowed it to increase training opportunities and pay employees more for their growing expertise, while still improving the company's overall financial results.

A completed example of the Cost of Employee Turnover Worksheet can be found in the Tools Section at the end of this chapter. For a blank template go to page 168. For a downloadable version go to www.LeadforGood.org. Every organization is different, but if yours experiences more than 25 percent turnover, it's worth completing this worksheet.

To calculate the rate of turnover, use the following formula: divide the total number of employees who left the organization in a 12-month period by the average total number of employees in that same 12-month period.

Rate of Turnover Calculation

$$\frac{\textbf{Total Number of Employees Who Left in a 12-month Period}}{\textbf{Total Average Number of Employees in the Same 12-month Period}} \times 100 = \%$$

Whether the reason for leaving was voluntary or involuntary, the total number who left the organization should be included in the calculation. Then you have a true picture of the turnover rate. Based on a 2010 study conducted by Opportunity Knocks, average turnover in the nonprofit sector is 16 percent.[3]

For example, fundraising professionals tend to leave every two years in search of higher paying opportunities. People tell me this is because they believe they have to move out to move up. Most nonprofit organizations don't establish a path of progression to entice successful fundraisers to stay. Funds raised by these KEY employees account for much of a nonprofit's overall financial health and are critical for stewarding relationships with donors. Losing these important players and the connections they make usually proves costly to an organization.

Once you've run the numbers, share with your board actual costs, both direct and indirect, of losing valuable employees. The operative word is valuable employee. Retaining poor performers isn't sound practice under any circumstance.

Nontraditional, Low-Cost Benefits to Offer Employees

For most nonprofits, employee pay will most likely be an issue. Social sector salaries are historically less than the private sector, but benefits packages tend to be more robust than their private sector counterparts. By adroitly communicating the value of the entire "package," the overall compensation your organization offers is much more competitive. Be sure to assign a dollar value to benefits such as vacation, sick leave, holidays, and the health plan. Consider adding nontraditional perks to your compensation package that promote quality of life. Many companies in the private sector may not offer benefits such as:

- Annual Wellness Program/Health Fair
- Dependent Care/Elder Care Referrals
- Compressed Work Week
- Telecommuting
- Flex Time
- Infants at Work
- Job Sharing
- Pets at Work
- Quiet Room

Work/Life Balance

People who work in the nonprofit sector commonly struggle to balance the demands of their work and home lives. That might be because that's what has always been expected, or perhaps in their drive to support their missions, nonprofit employees end up sacrificing themselves along the way. Nonprofit leaders' failure to find balance in their lives is costly. In 2013, the Meyer Foundation surveyed nearly 100 executive directors to determine how best to support them. Former Meyer Foundation President, Julie Rogers, noted "these people are sacrificing so much to take on the executive roles of these groups.

We are watching people not just burn out but make themselves sick in service to their communities."[4]

There is no magic formula for balancing your life, but understanding your priorities and taking time to enjoy yourself are key ingredients for improving how you feel and reducing your potential for burnout.

Wheel of Life

One way to gain clarity about your priorities is to complete a Wheel of Life exercise. This is by no means a new concept: it was originated by ancient Buddhists. Once you become clear on your priorities, then you can better focus on maintaining balance in your life. A blank template of the Wheel of Life can be found on page 208. For a downloadable version go to www.LeadforGood.org.

The Wheel of Life exercise asks you to look at various aspects of your life, including health, finances, romance, career, relationships with friends/family, spirituality, personal development, and physical environment.

On a scale of 1 to 10, rank how you are performing in each of the areas. The higher the number, the better you are doing. If there are areas of the wheel that have low numbers and are out of balance, then take steps to address those areas. Tackle just a few at a

Wheel of Life Tool

In this example, the individual has indicated she is satisfied with much of her life (scoring herself a 7 or better in most areas.) Where she sees a need for better balance (to make her wheel more circular and reduce "bumps" in her road of life) are in the areas of personal development and finances. She should complete the Personal Develepment Plan to determine the steps she intends to take over the next 12 months to improve her life balance.

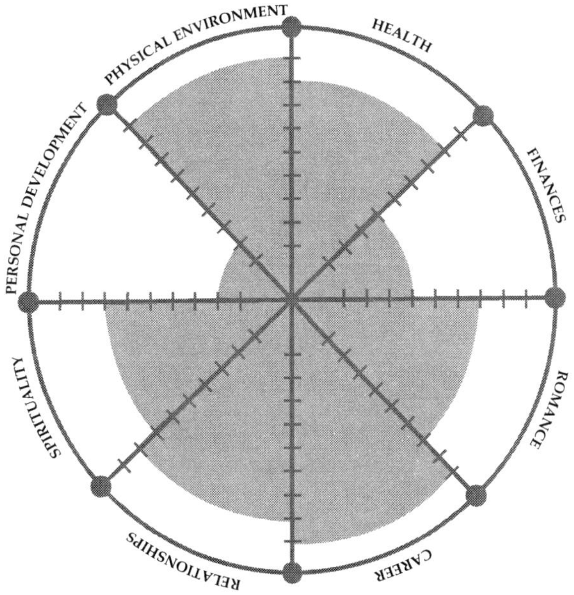

time. Use the Personal Development Plan introduced in Chapter One to list activities you intend to undertake to better balance your wheel.

The wheel didn't go out of alignment overnight, so regaining balance won't happen overnight. The plan should span a 12-month period. Look at the wheel again in one year's time to see how you are doing and tackle other issues that are still out of alignment.

An additional benefit of this exercise is that you will model how to achieve work/life balance for others, and you might attract a competent leader to succeed you when you are ready to leave. You will have demonstrated that your job may be done without burnout. You might consider conducting a work/life balance workshop each year for your staff, too. This is another no-cost, value-added perk with potentially high impact.

Finding Support

To help you find and keep a semblance of balance in your life, you should also identify an individual or group to support you in your journey. Many communities have groups of executive directors who meet on a regular basis to compare notes and discuss issues. These peer-networking organizations make a great place to find resources. Or, you might identify a respected colleague who would be interested in providing support to you in exchange for your support of him/her.

Another option is to find a trusted advisor to serve as a mentor. This should be someone you respect who has the expertise to guide you in decision-making. Look outside your board because boards change over time, and you don't want to risk the potential of being caught up in board politics.

You could also engage a professional coach to support you. A coach is different from a mentor. A mentor has subject matter expertise and provides advice to guide you as you navigate the leadership path. A coach is someone who asks powerful questions to help you access your creativity and resourcefulness as you set your own path. A coach helps you build awareness, assists in uncovering options, and provides support as you implement these choices. In "*Daring to Lead 2011: A National Study of Nonprofit Executive Leadership*," researchers found that of the more than 3,000 executive directors who completed the survey, 82 percent of those who had engaged a coach indicated coaching was an effective or very effective method of development.[5]

If you don't have a volunteer coach in the wings ready to provide support, you might want to check with your local chapter of the International Coach Federation (www.coachfederation.org) or its Foundation (www.foundation.coachfederation.org) to see if they coordinate pro bono coaching for nonprofit organizations in your area. Funders in your community might also be willing to underwrite the cost of coaching services.

If you decide to hire a coach, you should engage someone who is credentialed through the International Coach Federation (ICF.) That way, you will be assured your coach adheres to the standards and code of conduct developed for those in the profession. To find a credentialed coach, go to www.coachfederation.org. To help you select the right coach, use the Coach Interview Guide on page 163. For a downloadable version go to www.LeadforGood.org.

The most important element to consider when selecting a coach is whether he/she is a good "fit" with your personality. Do you feel comfortable with the coach and like her/his style? Do you believe he/she will be a strong partner? Ask for a commitment-free test run to determine

THE BENEFIT OF INVESTING IN SELF AND OTHERS

I took the reins as president of the Michigan Chapter of the National Multiple Sclerosis (MS) Society in July of 2007, aware that I had a challenging road ahead of me. This was my first experience leading a not for profit organization, and although I had inherited one with great bones, a strong and supportive national office, and a devoted board and staff, for several years the chapter hadn't been experiencing the level of financial growth necessary to maintain all of its commitments to its mission.

It became apparent that if I was going to be able to bring this great chapter back to full health, I had to make some really difficult and painful decisions, not the least of which included staffing changes. As I navigated these tough times, I was aware that I needed additional reinforcements - for me as a new leader, and also for my team.

It was an easy decision to reach out to a coach for guidance. I worked with Christina Pitts and her partner Lynne Aldrich at Pitts-Aldrich Associates, within my very limited budget, to provide learning opportunities and strengthen morale for the staff during my early years. The relatively small investment I made in my own personal coaching, and the time spent working on maintaining the morale of my team came back tenfold. Five years later, our success is measurable. Net results went from a 16.1 percent deficit, to a 12.5 percent surplus, and our revenue per employee has risen by 30.9 percent!

Elana Sullivan, President
National Multiple Sclerosis Society
Michigan Chapter

whether the person is right for you. In many cases, coaches are willing to conduct a complimentary session.

Learning Through Observation

Another method for investing in your own growth and development is to spend some time observing organizations with practices you would like to emulate. These can be groups in the same or different line of business. Most organizations would be honored by your request to observe them and discuss what makes them successful. You can also glean effective practices from reading some of the excellent books published in the last several years about successful organizational leadership. You can also find additional articles and resources at www.LeadforGood.org.

You can learn and grow by spending time working side-by-side with frontline employees and volunteers. If you work for a small organization, you have a ready opportunity. For larger organizations, you will likely need to create opportunities to work directly with frontline employees. The perspective you will gain is invaluable. It helps deepen your understanding of the organization's strengths as well as opportunities for growth. It gives you unique insight into constituents' unmet needs. It will also help you identify those who have potential as future leaders of your organization.

Giving Support

As important as it is to find sources of support for yourself, it is equally important that you provide development opportunities to your employees, key volunteers and board members. Giving support is an important part of becoming a great nonprofit leader. To make it happen means putting money into the budget for building the capacity of those in your organization. Rigorous defense of support dollars remaining in the budget will be necessary when the budget is under scrutiny. Do you have to invest a lot of money? No. Its intended use should be planned and clearly outlined.

Holding Meetings

Virtually every leader I've known groans about holding regular meetings. They believe meetings are a time-wasting practice that keeps them from serving the missions of their organizations. I would argue that regular meetings are one of the best investments a leader can make. Think back for a moment to the best boss you ever had. What made him or her so great? Did it have anything to do with how that person encouraged you? Gave you feedback that helped you grow? Provided opportunities to learn and expand your experience?

The *Field Guide* is intended to help you create a mechanism so that you can become that great boss. For some people, giving feedback on a consistent basis comes easily, whether it's positive or constructive. For most of us, however, it's not easy and it doesn't come naturally. Here's a straightforward way to create an effective feedback system for your nonprofit organization.

Start regular one-on-one meetings with those employees who report to you and insist that other leaders in your organization do the same with their direct reports. This means every employee in the organization (including key volunteers) is enjoying personal attention through face-to-face time with his/her supervisor. Half-hour meetings can happen as often as weekly or as infrequently as monthly. The meetings convey to employees that they are a priority. Therefore, meetings should only be postponed when absolutely necessary. By holding these meetings consistently, not cancelling or moving them around, you begin to form trust, and commitment and satisfaction improves. A blank template of Conducting Effective One-on-One Meetings can be found on page 166. For a downloadable version go to www.LeadforGood.org.

Meeting with board members one-on-one at least once a year is also a worthwhile investment. For key board members, such as the board chair, meeting for coffee or lunch once a quarter is appropriate.

The Take Away

Investing in yourself, as well as staff, key volunteers and the board, provides great returns for the organization. Putting processes in place to give and get regular feedback ensures all areas of the organization are aligned and functioning effectively. In addition, it minimizes burnout and turnover, prepares the next generation of leaders to step into more responsible roles, and allows the organization to better serve its mission.

TOOLS ● STEP 2
INVEST IN SELF AND OTHERS

EXAMPLE
COST OF EMPLOYEE TURNOVER WORKSHEET

HIRING ACTIVITIES	ESTIMATED TIME	COST
Ad in newspaper or online	Cost to write & place online and/or newspaper ad	$400
Application/resume review	6 hrs x hourly wage of reviewer	$ 87
Set-up interviews	2 hrs x hourly wage of scheduler	$ 20
Conduct interviews	8 hrs x hourly wage of interviewer	$116
Do background checks		
• Previous employer(s)	1 hrs x hourly wage of person conducting checks and/or fee for outside service	$ 10
• References	1.5 hrs x hourly wage of person conducting checks and/or fee for outside service	$ 22
• Credit history (if applicable)	0 hrs x hourly wage of person conducting checks and/or fee for outside service	$ 0
• Criminal record	Fee for outside criminal check service	$125
Conduct new hire orientation		
• Introductions to staff/equipment	2 hrs x hourly wage of person(s) conducting orientation plus hourly wage for new hire	$ 39
• Fill out new hire paperwork	2 hrs x hourly wage of person(s) conducting orientation plus hourly wage for new hire	$ 39
• Conduct required job training and policy review	4 hrs x hourly wage of person(s) conducting orientation plus hourly wage for new hire	$ 78
TOTAL FOR HIRING ACTIVITIES		**$1001**

COST OF EMPLOYEE TURNOVER WORKSHEET - Page 2

TERMINATION ACTIVITIES	ESTIMATED TIME	COST
Advice for "sticky" situations	Fees for professional counsel and Executive Director (ED) time	$375 $288
Payout of unused vacation/sick/PTO and/or severance (if applicable)		$ 0
Change locks, entry codes, computer passwords, etc.	2 hrs x hourly wage of person(s) responsible for computer administration plus fees for locksmith	$200
Paperwork • Prepare documentation of poor performance or misconduct • Create "off-cycle" paycheck	6 hrs x hourly wage of ED to prepare documentation Fees to create paycheck	$216
Communicate staffing change • Meet with employee w/witness to fire • Meet with staff to explain	1.5 hrs x hourly wage of ED and employee to do termination .5 hrs x hourly wage of ED and ALL 5 hrs unproductive time gossiping about event (assume 6 staff members)	$ 54 $108 $360
Unemployment payment expenses		$ 0
TOTAL FOR TERMINATION ACTIVITIES		**$1,601**

LOST PRODUCTIVITY	ESTIMATED TIME	COST
Overtime paid to staff to cover for work left undone by open position and/or new employee	160 overtime hrs x 1.5 hourly wage of person(s) working overtime to get job done	$2,880
Wages paid to new employee who is not yet productive	480 hrs x hourly wage of new hire while unproductive	$4,800
Time spent by other staff members training new employee	120 hrs x hourly wage of person(s) conducting training (plus hourly wage for new hire if not included above)	$1,440
Unproductive time spent by "lame duck" employee who has given notice	0 unproductive hrs x hourly wage of "lame duck"	$ 0
Burnout factor for current employees who are sick of having to train new employees and become either unproductive or quit	If enough turnover, may increase absenteeism among remaining employees and/or lose additional employees, etc.	$ 0
TOTAL COST OF UNPRODUCTIVE TIME		**$9,120**
TOTAL COST OF TURNOVER		**$11,722**

ASSUMPTIONS:

• ED = $45k or $21.50/hr
• Admin = $20k or $10/hr
• Dev Dir = $30k or $14.50/hr
• New Hire (Dev Dept Admin) $20k or $10/hr
• 6 Staff Members + ED + Dev Dir = 8 Total

CHAPTER THREE • STEP 3

THINK STRATEGICALLY

> A leader takes people where they want to go. A great leader takes people where they don't necessarily want to go but ought to be.
>
> Rosalynn Carter

Thinking strategically means thinking big picture. It means envisioning what could be rather than what exists at the moment. It means identifying a direction and shepherding the process to propel an organization toward achieving its purpose. Leaders need to do that. Leaders also need to clearly communicate that vision and inspire buy-in from others. Every individual activity the organization initiates must align with and support serving a unified mission and vision.

The strategic planning process is an excellent way to create and communicate an organization's direction. The process spells out specific activities it intends to execute to ensure delivery on the organization's promises. The best strategic plans include input from many sources, are specific, doable, and include measurable goals.

How does one begin creating a strategic plan? What are its disparate elements and how do all the pieces fit together? Envision a pyramid with the top representing an organization's vision. The vision clearly states the organization's purpose - why it exists. The next section represents the organization's mission - how the organization intends to accomplish its vision. Strategies follow. Some call strategies "goals" or "initiatives." Regardless, these are the over-arching activities an organization undertakes to accomplish its mission. Each element of the pyramid supports the next and ultimately aligns in perfect harmony with the vision.

Alignment Pyramid

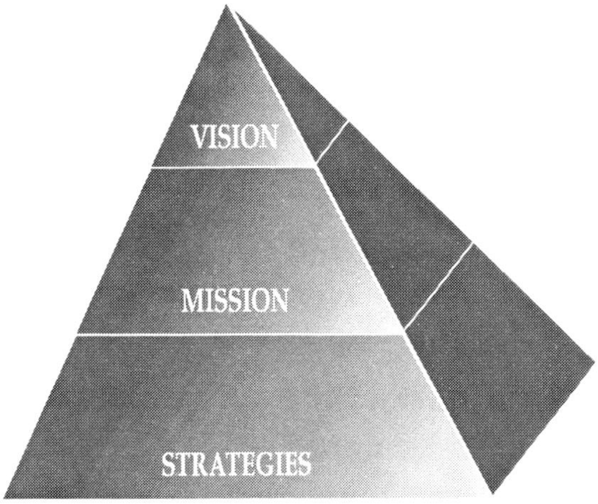

To help clarify each element involved in creating organizational direction and putting a comprehensive plan in place, let's explore each piece of the pyramid in sequence.

Vision

Every organization should develop a compelling vision statement. Vision describes the ultimate goal the organization is trying to achieve. The goal is lofty and often unattainable, yet it remains something to strive toward achieving. For example, Lead for Good's vision: "Every nonprofit organization thrives with great leadership" is succinct, memorable, and clearly conveys our nonprofit organization's purpose and what we are striving to achieve.

Developing an organization's vision statement is primarily the board of directors' responsibility in partnership with the chief executive. Generally, the vision is a permanent fixture unless the organization decides to change its reason for existing.

Mission

The mission statement explains why the organization exists and how it intends to achieve its vision. Lead for Good's mission is to "help individuals become great leaders so they are fully equipped to drive positive outcomes and sustain the missions of their nonprofit organizations. We develop effective nonprofit leaders through learning opportunities, peer-networking, mentoring and coaching." Like the vision statement, it should be succinct, memorable, and clear. Similarly to the vision, crafting the mission statement is the board of directors' responsibility in partnership with the chief executive.

Please note that vision and mission are sometimes described interchangeably depending on the source of the information. Regardless, each statement should be succinct and memorable.

Strategies

Strategies are key activities the organization chooses to implement to become sustainable and thrive. Strategies align with the vision and mission of an organization. You can think of strategies as "big buckets" that are filled with activities that support each strategy. Limit the buckets to no more than five. Although strategies will vary among organizations, based on size and where they are in their life cycle (i.e. start-up, growing, mature, declining), some examples of typical strategies include: increase sources of revenue, improve infrastructure, enhance marketing and brand recognition, and/or expand programs.

Tactics Support Strategies

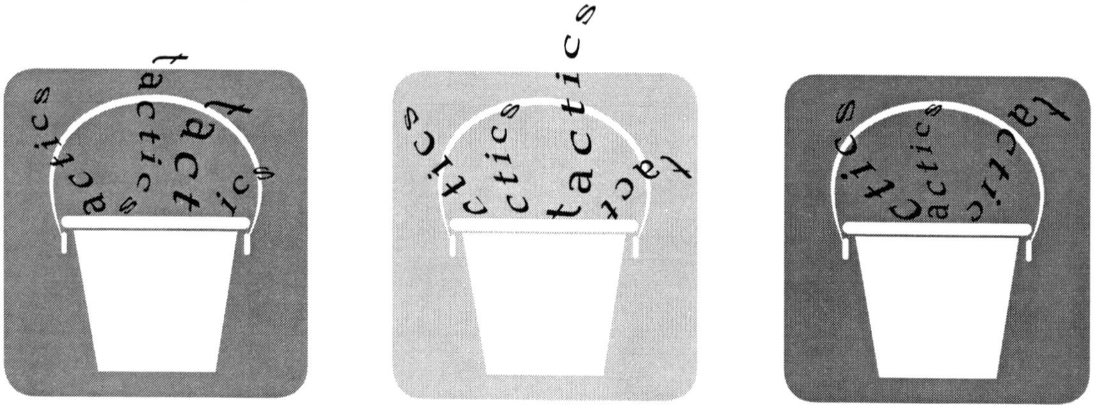

For each identified strategy, you and your board must determine a corresponding measurable goal. Goals need to be specific and achievable so that people understand expectations and funders understand the outcomes or impact you intend to accomplish. By setting clear goals, everyone works together toward the desired results. Make sure to create goals that stretch your organization. Jim Collins and Jerry Porras introduced the concept of a "big hairy audacious goal (BHAG)" in their article *"Building Your Company's Vision."*[6] The authors encourage organizations to define visionary goals that build on agencies passions, leverage their greatest unique strengths, drive their resource engine, are strategic and compelling and have a defined attainment date. Great BHAGs (pronounced bee-hag) serve as a unifying catalyst for change.

Creating the Game Plan

Engaging the board of directors and others in the strategic planning process is a critical component to creating a successful, thriving, sustainable organization. Setting the direction of the organization is a key responsibility of the board of directors.

Statistics indicate that upwards of 90 percent of strategic plans aren't executed. Plans sit on a shelf collecting dust because they don't include enough specificity to create a clear roadmap people can follow. To ensure you keep your eye on the prize, embed the activities the organization intends to do within the strategic plan. Then engage others to do much of the work. Spend your time with staff, facilitating the delivery of tasks rather than doing the work yourself.

When we revisit the pyramid, we see that these operational activities, in the form of tactics, action steps, and work steps, become the building blocks for delivering the organizations vision and mission. Be certain these tasks are aligned with your stated vision and mission. The more specific, measurable, and time-sensitive steps are, the more actionable the plan becomes.

Work Plan Pyramid

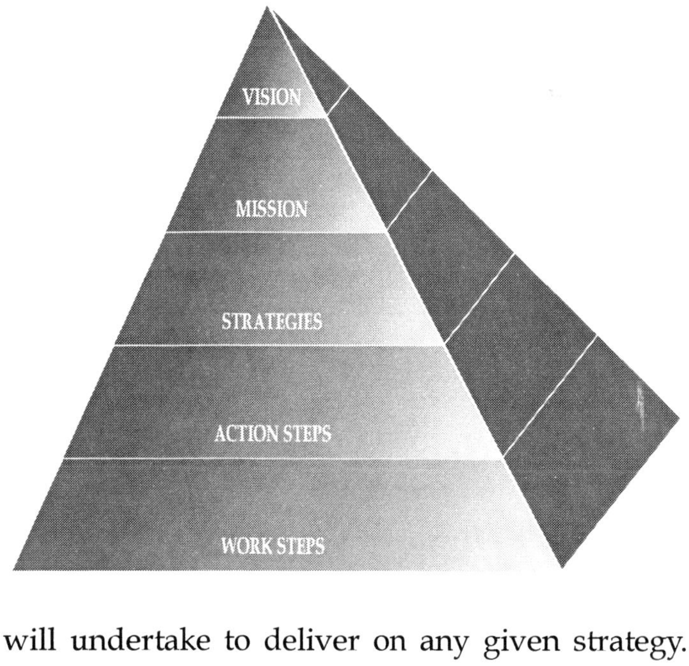

Tactics, Action Steps, and Work Steps

Tactics are major activities that support strategies. There are often a number of tactics an organization will undertake to deliver on any given strategy. Many of the tactics are project oriented. Make certain that each listed tactic supports the intended strategy's BHAG and that each is realistic. Assign responsibility and establish a time frame for delivery.

Action steps support tactics. To be manageable, tactics must be broken into smaller elements. Responsibility for managing action steps are often assigned to employees and are built into their job descriptions and/or performance reviews. This level of detail along with work steps are often referred to as the "work plan." It is this level of detail that helps ensure the strategic plan is actually executed. If there are no employees, action steps must be completed by the executive director or assigned to board members or trustworthy volunteers.

Work steps are even more bite-sized and manageable. These pieces of the plan outline the details of the action steps; the most specific components of a project. As much as possible, these tasks should be assigned to others to complete. Partner with your employees to create and solidify the tactics included in the plan, as well as to develop the action and work steps. Bear in mind that people who do the work are the ones who know best how to do it, so count on staff to provide details. If there is no staff, then you have no choice but to involve all resources at your disposal—board members and volunteers—to create the specific tasks around the plan. Regardless of who you engage to flesh out the steps, it is critical that this high level of detail is created.

Planning the Planning

We've talked about the *"what"* of thinking strategically; now let's tackle the *"how."* It's worth repeating that you need to involve the board, staff, and other key volunteers in the strategic planning process. I've known many CEOs who were reluctant to loosen their grips on the planning process. Control-driven methods don't allow others an opportunity to unleash their diverse perspectives and creative juices. Who you invite to the process is up to you and your board chair. Try to bring diversity to the table while keeping the team a manageable size. A group of more than 25 will be unwieldy. Use discretion when determining who to include. At a minimum, include your entire board and senior staff if your organization is large enough to have a leadership level. If you have fewer than 10 employees, include everyone in the process. Suggestions for one or two others to involve include:

- Committed volunteers
- Major funders

- Past recipients of support who you believe would add value to the process
- Partner agencies supportive of your organization's work

Being a great leader is about taking risks, and this is one of the occasions where stepping off the ledge into the abyss of others' ideas and perspectives is essential.

Timing the strategic planning process is another important element to consider. Initiate the process three to six months in advance of the budgeting process. This way, the initiatives' costs and revenue projections are built into the budget.

Working SMART

Simultaneous to determining individual plan elements, it is critical that each component therein be carefully considered, clearly defined, and assigned to an individual to manage. Each strategy, tactic, action step and work step must be created as a SMART goal. Components must be **S**pecific, **M**easurable, **A**chievable, **R**ealistic and **T**ime-sensitive. Identify who is taking responsibility for each component of your plan and how success will be measured. Establish a time frame for completion, determine what help you need, and reflect budget implications. I cannot overemphasize the importance of assigning responsibility for each element of the plan. There must be a process owner, someone who "owns" the execution of that element, to ensure it is completed. An example of a Strategic Planning Document can be found in the Tools Section at the end of this chapter. For a downloadable version go to www.LeadforGood.org.

Other Strategy-Related Components

Before putting strategic planning on the calendar or reserving space for a retreat, it is vitally important to determine whether the organization is READY to engage in a strategic planning process. Organizations should conduct an organizational assessment to determine their readiness and identify whether there are basic requirements that must be addressed before moving forward with strategic planning. If a nonprofit organization is relatively new or just starting, going through a strategic planning process will likely be overwhelming. It might be better to create a simple business plan that outlines the application process for attaining nonprofit status or create details around offering a single program.

The following lists the key areas that should be included in a thorough organizational assessment. This summary is adapted from the Checklist of Organizational Indicators produced by the Greater Twin Cities United Way.[7] A completed example of the Checklist of Organizational Indicators can be found in the Tools Section at the end of this chapter. For a blank template go to page 147. For a downloadable version go to www.LeadforGood.org. The assessment should be completed by staff, board, and other key stakeholders:

- Legal Indicators
- Financial Indicators
- Fundraising Indicators
- Human Resource Management Indicators
- Governance (Board) Indicators
- Volunteer Management Indicators
- Organizational Planning Indicators
- Program Planning Indicators
- Measurement Effectiveness Indicators

Once an organization determines its readiness and ability to move forward with strategic planning, it is important to gather information about what is happening locally, nationally and globally that will impact the organization's direction going forward. Referred to as an environmental scan, the data collected should be reviewed for trends related to economics, politics, technology, society, and the environment. This information should be shared with all parties invited to participate in the strategic planning process.

I recommend including two additional components in the strategic planning process. The first is the development of organizational values. Values define what the organization holds dear and defines how people associated with the organization are expected to behave. For example, an organization might decide one of its values is treating people with respect or that it values diversity or delivery on commitments. While not required, the process of identifying and defining values is catalyzing for an organization. People are more committed and engaged when an organization's values reflect their own personal beliefs.

The second component to include is determining an organization's primary customer. In his book, *The Practice of Management*, Peter Drucker introduces the concept. A primary customer is the singular, most important target group your organization serves.[8] Arriving at clarity about who is the key customer is not easy. You can only pick one. There has not yet been an organization I've worked with that didn't debate primary customer. Identifying the primary customer informs the development of your strategies and tactics.

A great example of the value of identifying the primary customer is found at St. Mary's Food Bank Alliance. The first food bank in the world, St. Mary's was founded in 1967 in Arizona by John van Hengel. In its first year, the organization distributed 250,000 pounds of food to those in need. In 2007 the group was struggling with the question about primary customer. Was its primary customer the hungry recipient of food, or was it the partner agencies who distributed the food? After much conversation and debate, the board and staff agreed: The primary customer was its partner agencies.

This represented a huge shift in thinking and, as you might imagine, heavily influenced the development of the nonprofit's three-year strategic plan. According to former St. Mary's Food Bank Alliance president and CEO, Terry Shannon, the focus on partner agencies had far-reaching, positive effects on the organization. By levering the power of its primary customer, the organization now distributes more than 72 million pounds of food per year.

Being Adaptable

The shifting global economy and quickly changing nature of our world necessitates frequent strategic plan review. When developing a plan, it is best to project out a maximum of three years, with focus on starting or completing activities within 12 to 18 months. A well-built strategic plan is designed as a living, breathing document. It must be reviewed and updated regularly at both board and staff meetings to remain relevant and dynamic.

When a new opportunity presents itself that supports the vision and mission of the organization, a thoughtful decision must be made about whether the organization has capacity to take on another program or project. Avoid piling on too many opportunities just because they become available.

You might have to decide to give up an existing initiative in order to create room to add another. Ultimately, it is your responsibility as leader to maintain balance and to seamlessly integrate additions.

Creating a Decision-Making Filter

A helpful tool in deciding whether to add a new initiative is a filter that asks key questions. Clarifying whether the project is the right fit also helps you avoid mission creep, a phenomenon caused by agreeing to add new programs because money is available, not because the program is aligned with the organization's vision or mission. While each organization needs to decide for itself what questions to ask when considering a new initiative, options include:

- Is this aligned with our vision, mission and values?
- Does it serve our primary customer?
- If not, does it serve as a relationship builder with an important constituency?
- Does it support a specific strategy?
- Is it a good use of limited resources?
- Is the social or financial impact favorable enough to replace an existing program?

A copy of the Decision-Making Filter can be found on page 174. For a downloadable version go to www.LeadforGood.org.

The Take Away

Engaging in formal planning that includes stakeholders is a vital component of

A SUCCESS STORY
HABITAT FOR HUMANITY AFFILIATE

One of the strongest, bravest strategic plans I've seen was developed by a large Habitat for Humanity affiliate. The organization had been challenged by its national office to grow substantially and to build 50 houses a year. At the time, it was building half as many. The organization had to completely rethink its approach to building affordable housing. Through a series of effective strategic planning exercises, they shifted their business model from a sub-division approach to an in-fill approach that allowed for the purchase of inexpensive land within an existing community. And, they decided to use new, multi-housing designs to supplement single-family dwellings. They also decided to create an indoor staging area so construction could continue year-round, allowing carpenters to work through extreme summer temperatures.

Each of the new tactics was fleshed out during staff planning sessions. The team wanted all new ideas and activities to happen immediately. That's where the concept of setting timeframes became really important. It was critical for staff to consider the wide breadth of activities planned throughout the organization. A visual that helped the group manage the enormity of the plan was a Gantt chart that showed timelines for each activity. Once staff realized that the bulk of their plan fell early in the three-year period, an effort was made to space actions more evenly over time. They were able to recognize that taking on everything at once was neither realistic nor doable.

To ensure employees gave full support to the strategic plan, the organization integrated specific action and work steps into each employee's annual performance review. This way, employees clearly understood how their jobs supported the organization's strategies. And, they were held accountable for delivering on expectations tied to the plan.

a successful, thriving, sustainable organization. Clear, specific communications about your plan is equally important. Keeping each other abreast of progress and adjustments ensures that the plan remains relevant.

To unleash the great nonprofit leader within, think strategically. Position yourself as the compass that sets the course for bringing your organization's mission and vision to fruition. Spend your leadership energies engaging others to deliver tactics, action steps and work steps. Doing so strengthens both you and your organization.

TOOLS ● STEP 3
THINK STRATEGICALLY

EXAMPLE
CHECKLIST OF NONPROFIT ORGANIZATIONAL INDICATORS

How to Use the Tool

The checklist indicators represent what is needed to have a healthy, well-managed organization. Since it is a self-assessment tool, organizations should evaluate themselves honestly against each issue and use the response to change or strengthen its administrative operations.

Ratings:

Each indicator is rated based on its importance to the operation and effectiveness of any nonprofit organization. The ratings are:

E: Indicators with an "E" are essential or basic requirements to the operations of all nonprofit organizations. Organizations that do not meet the requirements of these indicators could place their organizations in jeopardy.

R: An "R" rating signifies these indicators are recommended as standard practice for effective nonprofit organizations.

A: Additional indicators that organizations can implement to enhance and strengthen their management operations and activities are rated with an "A."

Checklist Responses:

Organizations can respond in one of three ways to each indicator used:

1. ***Needs work*** - An indicator is marked as "Needs Work" implies work has been done toward achieving this goal. The organization is aware of the need for this indicator, and is working toward attaining it.
2. ***Met*** - All indicators marked as "Met" demonstrate the organization has fulfilled an essential management need. However, the organization should review these indicators in the future to be sure its management remains

healthy in view of the many internal and external changes that occur in all organizations.

3. ***N/A*** - Indicators marked as "N/A" can mean several things, including:
   - The indicator is not applicable to the management operations of this organization.
   - The organization is not sure of the need to meet the requirements of this indicator.
   - The organization has not met, nor is it working on this indicator presently, but may address it in the future.

All organizations should take note: All responses to indicators should be reviewed carefully to see if they could improve management operations. Indicators checked "N/A" due to uncertain applicability to the organization must be further reviewed to determine if they should become a part of "doing business." If the assessors simply do not know what the indicator means, further information may be needed to accurately assess the feasibility of its application. Indicators marked "N/A" because they have not been met but that apply to the organization, may require immediate attention. Technical assistance, consulting, or training may be required to implement these indicators.

The indicators in this checklist should be informative and thought-provoking. The checklist can be used to achieve not only a beginning level of good management, but also improve existing management by providing the organization with greater stability, reliability and success in the nonprofit community. It is also a useful tool if an organization is experiencing management problems, to help pinpoint weaknesses so action can be taken or assistance sought to improve the organization's health. All organizations should use the checklist to re-assess themselves periodically to ensure compliance with established rules and regulations, and to continue improving administrative health through the indicator's helpful suggestions.

CHECKLIST OF NONPROFIT ORGANIZATIONAL INDICATORS - Page 3

Disclaimer

This checklist is designed to provide accurate and authoritative information regarding the topics covered. Legal requirements and non-legal administrative practice standards reflected herein are capable of change due to new legislation, regulatory and judicial pronouncements, and updated and evolving guidelines. All stated legal requirements are in effect as of October 2014. The same are utilized with the understanding that the provision of this checklist does not constitute the rendering of legal, tax or other professional services.

If the organization requires professional assistance on these or other nonprofit tax, management, or accounting issues, please contact your own professional advisors.

RATING	LEGAL INDICATORS	MET	NEEDS WORK	N/A
E	1. All relevant filings to the Secretary of State are current. These filings might include: Annual Registration, Articles of Incorporation with all amendments, Change of Corporate Name, Change of Corporate Address. (The particular state office that processes these filings depends on which state you live in.)	✓		
E	2. The organization is registered with and has filed its annual report with the Attorney General's Office. (The particular state office that processes these filings depends on which state you live in.)	✓		
E	3. The organization has filed the IRS form 1023 (application for 501(c) status, if applicable,) has received a letter of determination, and it is available for public inspection. This requirement applies to tax-exempt organizations.	✓		
E	4. IRS form 990 and 990T (unrelated business income) if required, have been filed and copies of the 990 are available to the public. This requirement applies to tax-exempt organizations.	✓		
E	5. Federal and state payroll tax withholding payments are current. This requirement applies to organizations with employees.	✓		
E	6. Quarterly and annual payroll report filings are current. This requirement applies to organizations with employees.		✓	

CHECKLIST OF NONPROFIT ORGANIZATIONAL INDICATORS - Page 4

RATING	LEGAL INDICATORS	MET	NEEDS WORK	N/A
E	7. The organization has filed with the appropriate State Economic Security agency and complies with all filing requirements of the State's Unemployment Fund. (This requirement varies among states. Contact the Attorney General's or Secretary of State's office for any filing requirements.)		✓	
E	8. If the organization has qualified employee health and retirement benefit plans, they meet all federal laws, including: COBRA; initial IRS registration; plan documents; annual filings of the 5500 C/R with copies available to employees. This requirement applies to organizations with employees.			✓
E	9. Organization acknowledges and discloses to its board and auditor any lawsuits or pending legislation which may have a significant impact on the organization's finances and/or operating effectiveness.	✓		
E	10. When the Board of directors makes decisions, a quorum is present and minutes are maintained.	✓		
E	11. If the organization is subject to sales tax, state and city filings and payments are current.		✓	
E	12. Organizations that participate in grassroots or direct lobbying have complied with all filings and government regulations.	✓		
E	13. Organizations that conduct charitable gambling have complied with government regulations.	✓		
E	14. Organizations with employees represented by a union must have copies of the union contracts on file.			✓
E	15. Organizations that operate in a fiscal or host-organization relationship with another organization or social service group have a written agreement on file.			✓

CHECKLIST OF NONPROFIT ORGANIZATIONAL INDICATORS - Page 5

RATING	GOVERNANCE (BOARD OF DIRECTOR) INDICATORS	MET	NEEDS WORK	N/A
E	1. The roles of the board and the executive director are defined and respected, with the executive director delegated as the manager of the organization's operations and the board focused on policy and planning.	✓		
R	2. The executive director is recruited, selected, and employed by the board of directors. The board provides clearly written expectations and qualifications for the position, as well as reasonable compensation.		✓	
R	3. The board of directors acts as governing trustees of the organization on behalf of the community at large and contributors while carrying out the organization's mission and goals. To fully meet this goal, the board of directors actively participates in the planning process as outlined in the planning sections of this checklist.		✓	
R	4. The board's nominating process ensures the board remains appropriately diverse with respect to gender, ethnicity, culture, economic status, sexual orientation, disabilities, and skills and/or expertise.		✓	
E	5. Board members receive regular training and information about their responsibilities.	✓		
E	6. New board members are oriented to the organization, including the organization's mission, bylaws, policies, and programs, as well as their roles and responsibilities as board members.		✓	
A	7. Board organization is documented with a description of the board and board committee responsibilities.		✓	
A	8. Each board member has a board operations manual.	✓		
E	9. If the organization has any related party transactions between board members or their family, they are disclosed to the board of directors, the Internal Revenue Service and the auditor.	✓		
E	10. The organization has at least the minimum number of members on the board of directors as required by its bylaws or state statute.	✓		
R	11. Bylaws conform to state statute and have been reviewed by legal counsel.	✓		

CHECKLIST OF NONPROFIT ORGANIZATIONAL INDICATORS - Page 6

RATING	GOVERNANCE (BOARD OF DIRECTOR) INDICATORS Continued	MET	NEEDS WORK	N/A
R	12. Bylaws include: a) how and when notices for board meetings are made; b) how members are elected/appointed by the board; c) what the terms of office are for officers/members; d) how board members are rotated; e) how ineffective board members are removed from the board; and f) a stated number or percentage of board members required for quorum to vote on policy decisions.	✓		
R	13. The board of directors reviews the bylaws annually or more often if needed.		✓	
A	14. The board has a process for handling urgent matters between meetings.		✓	
E	15. Board members serve without payment unless the agency has a policy identifying reimbursable out-of-pocket expenses.	✓		
R	16. The organization maintains a conflict-of-interest policy and all board members and executive staff review and sign annually to acknowledge and comply with the policy.	✓		
R	17. The board has an annual calendar of meetings. The board also has an attendance policy such that a quorum of the organization's board meets at least quarterly.		✓	
A	18. Meetings have written agendas and materials relating to significant decisions to be made are given to the board in advance of the meeting.	✓		
A	19. The board has a written policy prohibiting employees and members of employees' immediate families from serving as board chair or treasurer.		✓	
R	20. Board members annually commit to making a meaningful financial contribution, attending board meetings, and participating in organization-related events.		✓	
R	21. Board members complete two annual board assessments. The first pertains to the board as a group, and the second focuses on the performance of the individual board member.	✓		

CHECKLIST OF NONPROFIT ORGANIZATIONAL INDICATORS - Page 7

RATING	FINANCIAL INDICATORS	MET	NEEDS WORK	N/A
E	1. The organization follows accounting practices that conform to accepted standards.	✓		
E	2. The organization has systems in place to provide the appropriate information needed by staff and board to make sound financial decisions and to fulfill Internal Revenue Service requirements.	✓		
R	3. The organization prepares timely financial statements including the Balance Sheet (or Statement of Financial Position) and Statement of Revenue and Expenses (or Statement of Financial Activities) that are clearly presented and useful for the board and staff.	✓		
R	4. The organization prepares financial statements on a budget versus actual and/or comparative basis to achieve a better understanding of its finances.		✓	
E	5. The organization develops an annual comprehensive operating budget that includes costs for all programs, management and fundraising, all sources of funding, and is tied to the strategic plan. This budget is reviewed and approved by the board of directors.	✓		
R	6. The organization monitors unit costs of programs and services through the documentation of staff time and direct expenses and use of a process for allocation of management and general and fundraising expenses.		✓	
E	7. The organization prepares cash flow projections.	✓		
R	8. The organization periodically forecasts year-end revenues and expenses to assist in making sound management decisions throughout the year.	✓		
E	9. The organization reconciles all cash accounts monthly.	✓		
E	10. The organization has a review process to monitor that it is receiving appropriate and accurate financial information whether from a contracted service or internal processing.	✓		
E	11. If the organization has billable contracts or other service income, procedures are established for the periodic billing, follow-up and collection of all accounts, and has documentation that substantiates all billings.	✓		

CHECKLIST OF NONPROFIT ORGANIZATIONAL INDICATORS - Page 8

RATING	FINANCIAL INDICATORS Continued	MET	NEEDS WORK	N/A
E	12. Government contracts, purchase of service agreements and grant agreements are in writing and are reviewed by a staff member of the organization to monitor compliance with all stated conditions.	✓		
E	13. Payroll is prepared following appropriate state and federal regulations and organizational policy.		✓	
E	14. Persons employed on a contract basis meet all federal requirements for this form of employment. W-9s are completed by contractors and disbursement records are kept so 1099's can be issued at year end.		✓	
E	15. Organizations that purchase and sell merchandise take periodic inventories to monitor the inventory against theft, to reconcile general ledger inventory information, and to maintain an adequate inventory level.		✓	
R	16. The organization has a written fiscal policy and procedures manual and follows it.	✓		
E	17. The organization has documented a set of internal controls, including the handling of cash and deposits, approval over spending and disbursements.	✓		
E	18. The organization has a policy identifying authorized check signers and the number of signatures required on checks in excess of specified dollar amounts.	✓		
E	19. All expenses of the organization are approved by a designated person before payment is made.		✓	
R	20. The organization has a written policy related to investments.		✓	
R	21. Capital needs are reviewed at least annually and priorities established based on the strategic plan.		✓	
R	22. The organization has established a contingency plan identifying actions to take in the event of a reduction or loss in funding.	✓		
R	23. The organization has established, or is actively trying to develop, a reserve of funds to cover six months of operating expenses.		✓	
E	24. The organization has suitable insurance coverage, which is periodically reviewed to ensure the appropriate levels and types of coverage are in place.	✓		

CHECKLIST OF NONPROFIT ORGANIZATIONAL INDICATORS - Page 9

RATING	FINANCIAL INDICATORS Continued	MET	NEEDS WORK	N/A
R	25. Employees, board members and volunteers who handle cash and investments are bonded to help assure the safeguarding of assets.	✓		
E	26. The organization files IRS form 990's on a timely basis within prescribed time lines.		✓	
R	27. The organization reviews income annually to determine and report unrelated business income to the IRS.	✓		
R	28. The organization has an annual, independent audit of its financial statements, prepared by a certified public accountant.		✓	
R	29. In addition to the audit, the CPA prepares a management letter containing recommendations for improvements in the financial operations of the organization.		✓	
R	30. The board of directors, or an appropriate committee, is responsible for soliciting bids, interviewing auditors and hiring an auditor for the organization.	✓		
R	31. The board of directors, or an appropriate committee, reviews and approves the audit report and management letter and with staff input and support, and institutes necessary changes.	✓		
E	32. The audit, or an organization-prepared annual report that includes financial statements, is made available to service recipients, volunteers, contributors, funders and other interested parties.	✓		
R	33. Training is made available for board and appropriate staff on relevant accounting topics and all appropriate persons are encouraged to participate in various training opportunities.	✓		

CHECKLIST OF NONPROFIT ORGANIZATIONAL INDICATORS - Page 10

RATING	FUNDRAISING INDICATORS	MET	NEEDS WORK	N/A
E	1. Funds are raised in an ethical manner for activities consistent with the organization's vision, mission and strategic plan.	✓		
E	2. The board of directors and organization staff are knowledgeable about the fundraising process and the roles for fundraising in the organization.	✓		
E	3. The organization's board of directors has established a committee charged with developing, evaluating and reviewing fundraising policies and practices.	✓		
E	4. The committee is actively involved in the fundraising process and works to involve others on the board in these activities.		✓	
R	5. The board of directors, executive director and committee supports and participates in the total fundraising process, including project identification, cultivation, solicitation and recognition.		✓	
R	6. The fundraising program is staffed and funded at a level consistent with fundraising expectations.		✓	
A	7. There is direct communication and a strong relationship between marketing, accounting and other administrative support functions to assist in fundraising.		✓	
E	8. The organization is accountable to donors and other key constituencies and demonstrates its stewardship through regular communications and annual reports.		✓	

CHECKLIST OF NONPROFIT ORGANIZATIONAL INDICATORS - Page 11

RATING	USING AN OUTSIDE FUNDRAISER	MET	NEEDS WORK	N/A
A	1. The organization meets the nonprofit standards of the state charities review council (if one exists in the state, e.g., the Minnesota Charities Review Council provides standards for Minnesota's charitable nonprofits.)			✓
R	2. If the organization chooses to use outside professional fundraisers, at least three competitive bids are solicited. Each prospective outside fundraiser's background and references are checked.			✓
E	3. The organization insists on having signed, legally binding, mutually agreed upon agreements with outside professional fundraisers that outline each parties' responsibilities and duties, specifies how the contributed funds will be physically handled, and guarantees the fees to be paid meet the code of ethics outlined by the Association of Fundraising Professionals and are reasonable and fair.			✓
E	4. The organization has verified that the contracted fundraiser is registered as a professional fundraiser with the Attorney General, as required, and all filings necessary have been made before work commences.			✓
E	5. The fundraising committee or appropriate representatives from the board of directors review all prospective proposals with outside professional fundraisers and accept all agreements before they are signed.			✓
R	6. If the outside professional fundraiser plans to contact potential donors directly, the organization reviews the fundraising materials (e.g., public service announcements, print or broadcast advertisements, telemarketing scripts, pledge statements, brochures, letters, etc.) to verify their accuracy and to ensure the public disclosure requirements have been met.			✓
E	7. The organization properly reports all required information regarding use of outside professional fundraisers, amount of funds raised and the related fundraising expenses as required by state and federal law. The gross amount of funds raised by the contracted fundraiser is reported on the organization's financial statement. The fees and costs of the campaign are reported as an expense.			✓

RATING	HUMAN RESOURCE MANAGEMENT INDICATORS	MET	NEEDS WORK	N/A
	EMPLOYEES:			
E	1. The organization has a written personnel handbook/policy that is regularly reviewed and updated: a) to describe the recruitment, hiring, termination and standard work rules for all staff; b) to maintain compliance with government regulations including Fair Labor Standards Act, Equal Employment Opportunity Act, Americans with Disabilities Act, Occupational Safety and Health Act, Family and Medical Leave Act, Health Insurance Portability and Accountability Act (HIPAA,) Uniformed Services Employment and Reemployment Rights Act, Form I-9 and E-Verify, Affordable Care Act, and Affirmative Action Plan (if required), etc.		✓	
R	2. The organization follows nondiscriminatory hiring practices.	✓		
R	3. The organization provides a copy of or access to the written personnel policy to all members of the board, the executive director and all staff members. All staff members acknowledge in writing that they have read and have access to the personnel handbook/policies.		✓	
R	4. The organization has job descriptions including qualifications, duties, reporting relationships and essential functions.	✓		
R	5. The organization's board of directors conducts an annual review/evaluation of its executive director in relationship to a previously determined set of expectations.	✓		
R	6. The executive director's salary is set by the board of directors in a reasonable process and is in compliance with the organization's compensation plan.	✓		
R	7. The organization requires employee performance reviews be conducted and documented at least annually.	✓		
A	8. The organization has a compensation plan, and a periodic review of salary ranges and benefits is conducted.		✓	
A	9. The organization has a timely process for filling vacant positions to prevent an interruption of program services or disruption to organization operations.		✓	
A	10. The organization has a process for reviewing and responding to ideas, suggestions, comments and perceptions from all staff members.		✓	

CHECKLIST OF NONPROFIT ORGANIZATIONAL INDICATORS - Page 13

RATING	HUMAN RESOURCE MANAGEMENT INDICATORS Continued	MET	NEEDS WORK	N/A
	EMPLOYEES Continued:			
A	11. The organization provides opportunities for employees' professional development and training with their job skill area and also in such areas as cultural sensitivity and personal development.	✓		
A	12. The organization maintains contemporaneous records documenting staff time in program allocations.		✓	
	VOLUNTEERS:			
E	13. The organization has a clearly defined purpose of the role that volunteers have within the organization.		✓	
E	14. Job descriptions exist for all volunteer positions in the organization.		✓	
R	15. The organization has a well-defined and communicated volunteer management plan that includes a recruitment policy, description of all volunteer jobs, an application and interview process, possible stipend and reimbursement policies, statement of which staff has supervisory responsibilities over what volunteers, and any other volunteer personnel policy information.		✓	
E	16. The organization follows a recruitment policy that does not discriminate, but respects, encourages and represents the diversity of the community.		✓	
E	17. The organization provides appropriate training and orientation to volunteers to assist in the performance of their volunteer activities. Volunteers are offered training with staff in such areas as cultural sensitivity.		✓	
R	18. The organization is respectful of volunteers' abilities and time commitments and has various job duties to meet these needs.		✓	
R	19. The organization does volunteer performance appraisals annually and communicates to the volunteers how well they are doing, or where additional attention is needed. At the same time, volunteers are requested to review and evaluate their involvement in the organization and the people they work with and suggest areas for improvement.		✓	

CHECKLIST OF NONPROFIT ORGANIZATIONAL INDICATORS - Page 14

RATING	HUMAN RESOURCE MANAGEMENT INDICATORS Continued	MET	NEEDS WORK	N/A
	VOLUNTEERS Continued:			
R	20. The organization periodically provides volunteer recognition. Staff continuously demonstrates appreciation of volunteers and their efforts.		✓	
A	21. The organization has a process for reviewing and responding to ideas, suggestions, comments and perceptions from volunteers.		✓	
A	22. The organization provides opportunities for program participants to volunteer.	✓		
A	23. The organization maintains contemporaneous records documenting volunteer time in program allocations. Financial records are maintained for the volunteer time spent on programs and recorded as in-kind contributions.		✓	

RATING	OVERALL ORGANIZATIONAL PLANNING	MET	NEEDS WORK	N/A
E	1. The organization's purpose and activities meet community needs.		✓	
R	2. The organization frequently evaluates, by soliciting community input, whether its mission and activities provide benefit to the community.		✓	
R	3. The organization has a values statement that is reflected in the agency's activities and is communicated by its constituents.	✓		
A	4. The value statement includes standards of ethical behavior and respect for other's interests.	✓		
E	5. The organization has a clear, meaningful written mission statement that reflects its purpose and how it is delivered.	✓		
R	6. The organization has a clear, meaningful written vision statement that reflects what it ultimately strives to accomplish.	✓		

CHECKLIST OF NONPROFIT ORGANIZATIONAL INDICATORS - Page 15

RATING	OVERALL ORGANIZATIONAL PLANNING Continued	MET	NEEDS WORK	N/A
R	7. The board and staff periodically review the mission and vision statements and modify them to reflect changes in the environment.	✓		
E	8. The board and staff develop and adopt a written strategic plan to achieve its mission.	✓		
A	9. Board, staff, service recipients, volunteers, key constituents and general members of the community participate in the planning process.	✓		
E	10. The plan is developed by researching the internal and external environment.	✓		
R	11. The plan identifies changing community needs and leverages its strengths to better serve its constituents.	✓		
R	12. The planning process identifies critical issues facing the organization.	✓		
R	13. The plan identifies 3-5 strategies and creates specific measurable goals that address these critical issues.	✓		
E	14. The plan integrates all the organization's activities around a focused mission.	✓		
E	15. The plan prioritizes strategies and develops tactics, action steps, work steps and identifies process owners and timelines.	✓		
R	16. The plan establishes an evaluation process and performance indicators to measure progress toward achievement of strategies and goals and these results are reviewed regularly in board and staff meetings.		✓	
R	17. Through work plans (which include specific action steps), human and financial resources are allocated through the budgeting process to ensure accomplishment of strategies and goals within the allocated time frame.	✓		
A	18. The plan is communicated to all stakeholders of the organization -- service recipients, board, staff, volunteers and the general community.		✓	

CHECKLIST OF NONPROFIT ORGANIZATIONAL INDICATORS - Page 16

RATING	PROGRAMMING INDICATORS	MET	NEEDS WORK	N/A
E	1. Programs are congruent with the organization's vision, mission and strategic plan.	✓		
A	2. The organization actively informs the public about its programs and services.	✓		
A	3. Clients and potential clients have the opportunity to participate in program development.		✓	
R	4. Sufficient resources are allocated to ensure each program can achieve established goals.		✓	
R	5. Staff has sufficient training and skill level to produce the program.		✓	
A	6. Programs within the organization are integrated to provide complete services to clients.	✓		
R	7. Each program has performance indicators to ensure the program meets its goals.		✓	
R	8. Performance indicators are reviewed annually.		✓	
R	9. The agency collaborates with other organizations to produce the most comprehensive and effective services to clients.		✓	

RATING	MEASUREMENT EFFECTIVENESS INDICATORS	MET	NEEDS WORK	N/A
R	1. Every year, the organization evaluates its activities to determine progress toward strategy and goal accomplishment.		✓	
A	2. Stakeholders are involved in the evaluation process.		✓	
R	3. Evaluation includes a review of organizational programs and systems to ensure they comply with the organization's vision, mission, values, strategies and goals.		✓	
R	4. Results of the evaluation are reflected in the revised plan.		✓	
R	5. Periodically, the organization conducts a comprehensive evaluation of its programs. This evaluation measures program outcomes and impact.	✓		

Source: Adapted from checklist created by Greater Twin Cities United Way and edited by Carter McNamara, MBA, Ph.D.

EXAMPLE
STRATEGIC PLANNING DOCUMENT

✓		RESULTS EXPECTED (MEASURE OF SUCCESS)	TARGET DATES START/FINISH	PROCESS OWNER	ASSISTANCE REQUIRED/ RESOURCES AVAILABLE	BUDGET CONSIDERATIONS
	STRATEGY 1: IMPROVE ORGANIZATIONAL INFRASTRUCTURE	**Complete 95% of commitments on time and on budget**	**3/1 - 12/31**	**Laurie Nelson**		
	TACTIC 1: Enhance Administrative Processes	Improve efficiency to better serve constituents	By 8/1	Laurie Nelson		
	Action Steps: Install & maintain contact management database	Database installed	By 3/31	Laurie Nelson		$3000/yr
	Implement online file sharing platform	File sharing platform installed	By 4/30	Laurie Nelson	Board needs to sign up to receive access	N/C
	Hire Administrative Assistant for programs	New hire in place	By 6/30	Jordan Hale	Tina Wiles, Laurie Nelson, Tony Lewis	Approx. $25,000
	Work Steps: • Determine salary • Write job description • Develop new hire orientation plan • Post online at free nonprofit sites • Conduct interviews • Make offer		By 2/15 By 2/28 By 3/15 By 4/15 By 5/15 By 5/31	Jordan Hale Jordan Hale Tina Wiles Jordan Hale Jordan Hale Jordan Hale	Laurie Nelson	

STRATEGIC PLANNING DOCUMENT - Page 2

✓		RESULTS EXPECTED (MEASURE OF SUCCESS)	TARGET DATES START/FINISH	PROCESS OWNER	ASSISTANCE REQUIRED/ RESOURCES AVAILABLE	BUDGET CONSIDERATIONS
	TACTIC 2: Increase Engagement of Board of Directors	100% board participation in at least one event each year	By 12/31	Yvonne Jones (Board Chair)	Laurie Nelson and members of Board of Directors	
	Action Steps: Review and sign board commitment agreement annually	All board members sign agreement	By 1/31	Laurie Nelson	Yvonne Jones and all board members	
	Develop a board orientation plan	Begin orientation for all new board members	By 4/1	Yvonne Jones	Laurie Nelson	
	Provide board learning opportunities	Training session held at least once per year	By 12/31	Yvonne Jones	Governance Consultant	$1200
	STRATEGY 2: DEVELOP PRODUCTS AND SERVICES	**Add a new product or services that meets constituent needs**		**Jordan Hale**		
	TACTIC 1: gather feedback from constituents	Identify key new program to launch	By 1/15	Jordan Hale	Marketing Consultant and Laurie Nelson	$4000
	Action steps: Create and send RFP for marketing consultant	RFP distributed to preferred vendors	By 8/30	Laurie Nelson	Jordan Hale	
	Select marketing consultant	Selection process completed	By 10/15	Laurie Nelson	Jordan Hale	
	Identify key constituents to interview 1-on-1	Interviews completed	By 11/15	Laurie Nelson	Jordan Hale and Yvonne Jones	
	Identify key constituents to invite to focus group	Focus group held	By 11/30	Laurie Nelson	Jordan Hale and Yvonne Jones	
	Identify constituents to send survey	Responses tabulated	By 11/30	Laurie Nelson	Jordan Hale and Yvonne Jones	

CHAPTER FOUR • STEP 4

INSPIRE OTHERS

Experts who focus on leadership talk about the importance of being inspirational. What does that mean exactly, and how does one become an inspirational leader? For some, it seems to come naturally and without effort. For most of us, being inspirational takes energy and thoughtful action. This chapter focuses on techniques and tools to help you become an inspiration to others.

> If your actions inspire others to dream more, learn more, do more and become more, you are a leader.
>
> John Quincy Adams

Building Trust

Leaders' actions and behaviors set the tone for how others behave, which ultimately defines the culture of an organization. In his book, *The Speed of Trust*, Stephen M. R. Covey asserts, "The ability to establish, extend, and restore trust with all stakeholders - customers, business partners, investors and coworkers - is the key leadership competency of the new, global economy."[9] By consistently demonstrating and modeling trustworthy behavior, a leader creates a culture of trust within an organization.

One way to achieve trust is to frame your behavior as a value. In this instance, the value of trust defines how you operate as an individual. To have meaning and impact, and translate to inspiration, your value must be clear to you and others and be unwavering in practice. Creating trust requires ethical practice, integrity, and service excellence.

Ethical practice is defined as conforming to accepted standards of conduct. It means doing the right thing as defined by the constructs of society, which creates consistency. Integrity is also about consistency and setting a standard, and always following your own moral compass. **Integrity** means that others can rely on consistency in the decisions you make and the direction you set as a leader. You determine the standard and define what is "doing the right thing" based on your inner code of conduct.

Service excellence completes the triad of values essential to building trust and inspiring others. In the private sector, how we are treated as customers impacts how we feel about a company and whether we will be loyal to it or look elsewhere to fulfill our needs. Nonprofits are no different; they also provide products and services. How employees of a nonprofit treat recipients of services or other stakeholders is a direct reflection on leadership.

If your organization provides excellent service, then constituents will see you as someone who is committed to "doing the right thing." This fuels your reputation as an ethical leader who has integrity. Providing excellent service applies equally to the organization's internal and external customers. By demonstrating to staff and volunteers that you care about them as much as you care about external customers, you will further build commitment and serve as an inspiration to others.

Building a Culture of Service Excellence

Strong leaders empower employees to resolve issues, use service missteps as learning opportunities, and celebrate service successes publicly within the organization. Including a service measure in employees' performance reviews re-enforces employees' efforts to provide excellent customer service.

There are myriad ways to begin building or strengthening a culture of service excellence. Take every opportunity to clearly articulate your organization's commitment to providing excellent service. Consider adopting this concept as an organizational value (in addition to an individual value) and include it in the orientation process with new employees. Also, keeping a log of concerns and/or complaints received from external customers will help you identify trends and ensure that all issues are addressed. The log should include the following: date, name of person/organization involved, issue, who within the organization was assigned to resolve the issue, and ultimately when and how the issue was resolved. Based on the number of concerns/complaints, review the log at leadership meetings to ensure every issue is resolved and that changes to correct the situation are implemented. This strategy avoids future mishaps and makes for more satisfied recipients of service. A completed example of the Service Issues Log can be found in the Tools Section at the end of this chapter. For a blank template go to page 199. For a downloadable version go to www.LeadforGood.org.

To strengthen satisfaction among your employees and volunteers, adopt an internal process that acknowledges them. They should be recognized for providing excellent service and support to others both inside and outside the organization. Consider an "I Appreciate" Program to nominate people to be named employees of the month in various categories or simply as a way for people to recognize one another with no award attached. A completed example of an "I Appreciate" can be found in the Tools Section at the end of this chapter. For a blank template go to page 179. For a downloadable version go to www.LeadforGood.org.

Finally, consider conducting mini-workshops to remind employees and volunteers about the importance of providing excellent service. Ask them to think of a time they received great service and how that impacted them. Invite clients of the organization to share their experiences regarding customer service.

Ensuring Cultural Competence

Understanding, valuing, and championing diverse perspectives is also an important element of building trust and inspiring others. According to Terrry Cross, Barbara Bazron, Karl Dennis and Mareasa Issacs, cultural competence is, "a set of congruent behaviors, attitudes, and policies that come together in a system, agency, or among professionals and enable [them] to work effectively in cross-cultural situations."[10] While there are many definitions of culture, in Cross, et al, "culture" implies "the integrated pattern of human behavior that includes thoughts, communications, actions, customs, beliefs, values, and institutions of a racial, ethnic, religious, or social group."[11] Culture is fluid; it is constantly changing depending on outside influences and social shifts within a specific population. In other words, what's true now might not be true in the future.

Leaders demonstrate cultural competence in many ways. Coming to decisions and opinions from a position of curiosity and openness is a necessary element. Seeking to understand diverse perspectives and beliefs of others is also key. Learning to appreciate and invite differences and being aware of how your own cultural values influence your view of the world is also important. And finally, culturally competent, inspirational leaders remain flexible and gracefully adapt to fit shifting contexts.

MINI ACTIVITY
ARE YOU CULTURALLY COMPETENT?

Consider the following statements to get a sense of your level of cultural competence. These are just a few of 37 included in a self-assessment checklist created by the National Center for Cultural Competence at Georgetown University.[12] This assessment was created specifically for healthcare workers, but is applicable to anyone.

A = Things I do frequently, or statement applies to me to a great degree
B = Things I do occasionally, or statement applies to me to a moderate degree
C = Things I do rarely or never, or statement applies to me to minimal degree or not at all

_____ I avoid imposing values that may conflict or be inconsistent with those of cultures or ethnic groups other than my own.

_____ I intervene in an appropriate manner when I observe other staff or clients within my program or agency engaging in behaviors that show cultural insensitivity, racial biases and prejudice.

_____ Even though my professional and moral viewpoints may differ, I accept individuals and families as the ultimate decision-makers for services and supports impacting their lives.

The entire self-assessment can be found on page 170. For a downloadable version go to www.LeadforGood.org.

Admitting Mistakes and Taking Ownership of Difficult Decisions

To be truly inspirational, one must be willing to admit mistakes. Everybody makes them, but how you handle them hugely impacts the way people judge your character. We've all worked with people who won't apologize or admit making an error.

This behavior is often caused by a lack of confidence more than anything else. If you ever hope to create an organizational culture based on mutual respect and trust, you must be willing to take responsibility for mistakes.

MY BEST BOSS
THE CONSUMMATE LEADER

The epitome of a great inspirational leader is Gretchen Shine. She was the best boss I ever had. Gretchen consistently demonstrated the ability to motivate, educate, support and inspire not only me, but everyone else who worked for her. During her 20+ years as a senior executive at a Fortune 500 company, Gretchen managed a team of nearly 200 employees. She enjoyed a single-digit turnover rate.

One of her greatest strengths was her ability to clearly articulate her thoughts and to actively listen to the thoughts of others. Gretchen's winning approach included giving gentle, yet specific corrective feedback, using mistakes as opportunities to learn, freely admitting her own mistakes, and giving credit where credit was due. Staff, including me, was inspired to push our limits and stretch to do anything Gretchen asked. It was part of her larger plan to lay groundwork and build her teams' leadership skills with the specific intent of helping us get promoted.

By focusing on inspiring her internal customers (her employees) Gretchen's leadership directly resulted in better service for external customers. This translated into increased profitability and customer service accolades. We all won.

A great leader is also willing to make tough decisions, whether this is to embark on a new organizational direction, reallocate resources, or opt not to pursue a new program that would bring in much needed revenue, but is not aligned with the vision and mission of the organization. Conflict is a natural by-product of strong decision-making. How you handle the communication process makes all the difference in how well a shift in direction or other issue is received by those who are affected by the decision.

Implementing Effective Communications

Being an effective communicator is a KEY attribute that unlocks the great nonprofit leader within. Whether it's talking to someone one-on-one, sharing news with your organization, or advocating on behalf of your cause, what you say, how you say it, and when you say it all contribute to your ability to inspire others.

Effective one-on-one communication is important if you want to be trusted and admired as an inspirational leader. This is an area that may not be delegated to someone else on your behalf. Part of being a great leader is addressing individuals honestly and directly in a timely manner, whether you are conveying good news or bad news. In fact, the sooner a bad news issue is addressed, the less time there is for problems to grow and fester.

When addressing conflict one-on-one or when it is necessary to have a difficult conversation, refer to the following tips:

- Don't enter into a conversation while angry; consider this an opportunity to improve the work environment, not a gripe session.
- Set up the conversation by saying "I have a difficult situation I need to discuss with you. Is this a good time for us to meet?"
- When preparing for the discussion, be clear on FACTS and don't make assumptions.
- Come from a position of curiosity; ask yourself "Why would a reasonable person do/say this?" and be open to learning why.
- When sharing your concerns or perspective, speak in terms of "I" not "you."
- Pay attention and make eye contact.
- Be respectful and don't interrupt.
- Build on what has been said.
- Focus on issues that are solvable.
- Listen for understanding rather than thinking about your response.
- If you receive constructive feedback, say "thank you."

This list of tips for Addressing Conflict One-on-One can be found on page 137. For a downloadable version go to www.LeadforGood.org.

Improving Communications by Using Emotional Intelligence

To become a successful communicator, it is important that you identify and deal with the emotions of others as well as manage your own feelings, especially when dealing with an emotionally-charged situation. Effective dialogue occurs when people bring mutual purpose, mutual respect and mutual meaning to a difficult conversation. One proven technique is to train yourself to focus on facts while attempting to resolve an issue. For example, when dealing with a staff member who is chronically late, I would say something like "I notice you have been at least 15 minutes late for three of the last 10 days" rather than "You are late all the time."

It's advantageous to quiet assumptions and give the person in question the benefit of the doubt about the reason(s) an issue is occurring. In the same example, I might incorrectly assume the person is late because she doesn't care about her job or she is lazy and can't drag herself out of bed in the morning. However, by coming from a position of curiosity and asking about the cause of her tardiness, I might learn that her mother is in the hospital. She's late because she is rushing to work from a bedside morning visit. Holding emotions and negative assumptions in check creates an opportunity to empathize and build a stronger bond with an employee. The stage is then set to work together to develop a mutually acceptable solution. I don't hurt her feelings, she doesn't view me as a cold-hearted boss, and the problem is successfully solved.

The idea of emotional intelligence was first described by Edward Thorndike in the 1930s. However, the concept did not gain popularity until 60 years later. In 1990, Peter Salovey and John D. Mayer developed a model that identified four factors of emotional intelligence:

1. **Perceived Emotions:** This often involves identifying nonverbal cues such as body language, facial expressions, or tone of voice.

2. **Reasoning with Emotions:** This generates thinking about and prioritizing reactions. In other words, focusing on those things that capture your attention.

3. **Understanding Emotions:** This allows you to be open to what the emotions of others might mean (such as in the example of why the employee is late.)

4. **Managing Emotions:** This enables you to regulate your emotional response and be both graceful and effective in handling a potentially unpleasant situation.[13]

Most experts agree that emotional intelligence can be learned and improved through practice. How strong is your emotional intelligence? For more information about how to measure and enhance your skills in this area, excellent resources can be found at www.talentsmart.com.

Stop, Challenge, Focus is a proven technique designed to help discharge a build-up of emotion. This is especially helpful when tempers are high and an immediate response is required.

Stop means realizing that you are in stress and levying a self-imposed "time out." Identifying when you are angry is crucial if you hope to control your emotions and have a productive conversation with someone. **Challenge** refers to engaging in self-talk to acknowledge to yourself how and why the situation has upset you. It also means consciously deciding not to let the situation get to you and resolving to abandon your anger or frustration. **Focus** is about moving forward with a commitment to truly listen to what the other person is saying, and productively working to address their needs, wants and concerns. A copy of the Stop, Challenge, Focus Tool for Leaders can be found on page 200. For a downloadable version go to www.LeadforGood.org.

Effective organizational communications occur when information is disseminated quickly, succinctly and transparently to all the appropriate stakeholders of your organization. When something happens that has an impact on the agency, time is of the essence in communicating it to others who should know about it. This is a pivotal opportunity to demonstrate trust - tell all those who would want to know about the information and ask them to maintain confidentiality if that is what's warranted. Take responsibility for sharing as quickly and openly as possible, especially when it is bad news. When something goes wrong, or a change is being made or a sticky situation arises, if it's not addressed swiftly and directly by the leader, people tend to speculate to fill the information void.

As the leader, you are not only responsible for your own communication approach, you also determine the communication culture of the organization. The way you conduct yourself has much to do with setting the stage for how others in your organization communicate with one another.

One way to influence the communication culture is to ensure meetings are meaty and generative. Nothing drains limited resources from an organization more than disorganized, haphazard meetings. Establishing a framework—protocols— for meetings allows staff, board members and other volunteers to participate in healthy exchanges of information and productive work.

When planning and conducting a meeting, refer to the following Meeting Protocol Suggestions:

- Create and send out an agenda, reports and any required reading a few days in advance.
- Set ground rules for behavior while participating in meetings. A copy of Ground Rule Options for Meetings can be found on page 178. For a downloadable version go to www.LeadforGood.org.
- Use a parking lot (a blank piece of paper taped to the wall) to capture unrelated issues that arise during the meeting. Review and address/assign the items in the parking lot at the end of the meeting in order to stay on track.
- Have minutes with action items including names and dates of commitments.
- Send minutes out within 48 hours after the meeting to give time for people to act on their commitments (if practical and appropriate.)
- For board meetings, create a consent agenda to dispense with wasting time reviewing minutes and other documents that do not require discussion. A copy of possible Consent Agenda Elements can be found on page 167. For a downloadable version go to www.LeadforGood.org.

A copy of Meeting Protocol Suggestions can be found on page 184. For a downloadable version go to www.LeadforGood.org.

If your organization has a strategic plan, be sure to include a discussion about the plan on the agenda, or at a minimum include updates in the consent agenda materials. By reviewing elements of the plan on a regular basis, whether at board meetings, staff meetings or volunteer meetings, accountability is increased for those responsible for its execution. In addition, regular review ensures the plan remains a living, breathing roadmap that benchmarks progress.

For the board, an effective way to ensure the strategic plan is integrated into meetings is to align board committees with the established strategies of the organization. For example, you might name a committee "Enhancing Infrastructure," because that is a strategy outlined in the organization's plan. Board members serve as chairs of these committees and are responsible for owning/facilitating implementation of each of the strategies. They are also charged with reporting to peers about progress.

Advocating on Behalf of Your Cause

Helping others outside your organization understand and support your cause is the third major component of effective communications. Clearly articulating to the community, state, country and/or world the value of supporting your organization's particular mission and vision is critical to ensure sustainability. Leslie Crutchfield and Heather McLeod Grant, in their book *Forces for Good*, describe high impact organizations as those that advocate in addition to providing products and services.[14]

Sometimes there is confusion around the term advocacy in the nonprofit sector. According to an article entitled *"Lobbying and Advocacy - Similarities and Differences,"* when nonprofit organizations advocate on their own behalf, they are looking to influence some element of society, such as encouraging individuals to change their behavior or educating employers about the impact of their rules. Lobbying, on the other hand, refers specifically to advocacy efforts that attempt to influence legislation. This distinction is important because laws limiting lobbying done by nonprofits do not govern their other advocacy activities.[15]

While much has been written about lobbying in the nonprofit sector, there continues to be confusion around what are acceptable practices when interacting with legislators; practices that avoid problems with the IRS and the potential of jeopardizing tax exempt status.

In fact, a limited amount of lobbying by nonprofits is acceptable according to *"Advocacy Rules for Nonprofits"* published by Independent Sector. "In general, nonprofit organizations described under Section 501 (c)3 of the tax code may engage in lobbying and other advocacy activities within certain limits."[16]

Acceptable legislative activities for nonprofits include:

- Providing technical assistance or advice to a legislative body or committee in response to a written request.
- Making available nonpartisan analysis, study or research.
- Providing examinations and discussions of broad, social, economic and similar problems.

- Communicating with a legislative body regarding matters that might affect the existence of the organization, its powers and duties, its tax-exempt status, or the deduction of contributions to the organization (the "self-defense" exception.)
- Updating the members of your own organization on the status of legislation, without a call to action.[17]

A copy of the Legislative Activities Acceptable for Nonprofits can be found on page 181. For a downloadable version go to www.LeadforGood.org.

With the exception of churches, if a nonprofit organization wants to engage in more lobbying activities than permissible for a 501 (c)3 organization, an option is to change its status to operate under Section 501(h) of the tax code. Check with a tax advisor or attorney on whether this approach is appropriate for your organization.

Making Effective Presentations

Whether it's sharing information with legislators or communicating to other groups inside or outside your organization, people worry more about speaking in public than they do about dying. To be an inspirational leader, it is critical to be able to clearly and passionately convey messages of import (or find someone who will serve as the spokesperson on your behalf.) Delivering a compelling message is how individuals are inspired to take action and support your mission.

One way to hone your oratory skills is to videotape yourself making a speech, critiquing your performance, and making adjustments as necessary. Another option is to conduct a presentation in front of two or three trusted advisors who are willing to give honest feedback and help you tweak your presentation style. If public speaking is really unnerving, I suggest you try www.toastmasters.org to find resources to support you. A Presentations Skills Checklist to use when critiquing a presentation can be found on page 194. For a downloadable go to www.LeadforGood.org.

In *"Write A Great Talk in 12 Easy Steps,"* Mandy Bass provides an outline to create an effective presentation. The steps include:

1. Know your desired outcome before you create your presentation.
2. Understand your audience and how your talk fits.

3. Make the connection between what you are saying and what the audience needs/wants.
4. Clarify your win/win outcome for the audience.
5. Learn the specific parameters and criteria like number of people in the audience.
6. Brainstorm your ideas about what you want to say and be sure to include stories.
7. Organize your ideas into an outline.
8. Write the body of the presentation.
9. Create an enticing "ad" that summarizes the main points to use as a teaser.
10. Create visual aids and handouts that engage the audience - focus on pictures, not words, and create opportunities for audience participation.
11. Plan the opening - it's always good to start with a story.
12. Create the close - it's always good to summarize and end with a story.[18]

The full article with a more detailed explanation of each of the components of *"Write a Great Talk in 12 Easy Steps"* can be found on page 210. For a downloadable version go to www.LeadforGood.org.

Acknowledging Others

In *Good to Great*, Jim Collins identifies humility as a characteristic of a top-notch leader.[19] One way to demonstrate humility is by making sure you give credit to others where credit is due. It also means acknowledging people in a meaningful way, whether they are employees, partners, donors or volunteers. While some people respond positively to public accolades, others prefer quiet acknowledgement without fanfare.

Recognize others the way they want to be recognized. One method for getting clear about how best to acknowledge a person is to ask directly about his/her preferences. This can be done informally as part of a conversation or as a survey sent to key stakeholders. Either publicly or in private, a good, old-fashioned, sincere, specific "THANK YOU" that names their achievement is always a great way to recognize outstanding effort. Diversify the way you recognize achievement. You can communicate your appreciation in person, voicemail, handwritten note, e-mail, certificate, food, small gift with the organization's logo, balloons, flowers, lunch, or any other way your VIP has identified he/she would like to be acknowledged.

Mary Kay Ash, founder of the Mary Kay cosmetics empire, spoke wisely when she said, "Everyone has an invisible sign hanging from their neck saying, 'Make me feel important'." Making time for the people in your organization says they are important to you. Practice "MBWA" (Management By Walking Around.) Make it a point to check-in or say hello to everyone in the office or in your area each day you are there. If you have multiple sites, than make it a point to visit all of them regularly.

Taking the time to connect on a personal level with your staff, board members, other key volunteers and donors is another way to acknowledge their importance to your organization. Ask about their families, hobbies, favorite sports, and vacations. It shows you're interested in who they are, not just what they do to support the organization. By actively listening to what they say, you are sending the message that the person is important. If you have a lousy memory like me, you may want to make a note of those details for future reference.

The Take Away

Being an inspirational leader doesn't come naturally to most of us. It takes hard work. It means being unwavering in your commitment to your values, making and communicating tough decisions, effectively articulating your vision and mission, advocating about it passionately and persuasively, addressing issues quickly and effectively, managing your own emotions, admitting when you make a mistake, and giving credit where credit is due.

TOOLS ● STEP 4
INSPIRE OTHERS

EXAMPLE
SERVICE ISSUES LOG

DATE	NAME/ ORGANIZATION OF PERSON WITH ISSUE	ISSUE DESCRIPTION	ISSUE ASSIGNED TO	WHEN & HOW ISSUE RESOLVED
12/1/16	Philip Jones	Never received notification whether he was approved for services.	Glenda B.	Letter never generated to notify Mr. Jones he had been approved. Letter sent on 12/4/16 indicating he could begin receiving services.
3/12/17	Tina Harkins	Called to complain about service received from Belinda Tanner who works in client services. Ms. Harkins says she was rude and condescending.	Glenda B.	Discussed situation with Belinda and she admitted she got frustrated because Ms. Harkins appeared drunk when she called. Her words were slurred and she was hard to understand. After following up with Ms. Harkins, it was learned she has Parkinson's and that is why her words were slurred. A notation was put on her account indicating this disability. Belinda was both embarrassed and apologetic. She called Ms. Harkins on 3/13, apologized and gave her a direct phone number to use to call her any time she needed help in the future.
7/2/17	Bill Cacmus	Suggested a process improvement regarding delivery of service.	Tonya F.	In process of implementing change based on client's recommendation. Should be in place by end of year 2017.

EXAMPLE
I APPRECIATE...

NAME: *Glenda Billings*

Because she/he: *Did an excellent job addressing the concerns of a client named Philip Jones. Not only did she meet his needs, she went above and beyond, and arranged for his first series of appointments so that no time would be lost when sending the letter saying he was approved for service. He could simply bring the signed document to his first appointment rather than following the regular protocol of sending in the signed document and then receiving a follow-up call from us.*

And because of that: *Mr. Jones called back in and complimented the organization on doing such a great job being responsive and supporting him.*

And because of that: *He said he would recommend our organization to others who needed support and he would be happy to write a testimonial about the high quality of service he has received.*

Which resulted in: *Mr. Jones being included as a presenter at our Spring Fundraising Event where he spoke about the value of our organization based on his own experience. We raised more than $300,000 at the event.*

CHAPTER FIVE • STEP 5
SHARE LEADERSHIP

The ability to share leadership is another of the key skills a nonprofit executive must demonstrate to be successful. While shared leadership, also referred to as diffused or collective leadership, isn't unique to nonprofits, it plays a much more prominent role than it does in the private sector. This approach to leadership requires leaders to partner with and empower others and ultimately give power rather than withhold it. Adopting this philosophy is critical if a leader hopes to secure funding, engage board members and key volunteers, partner with other organizations and wring out the most productive use of limited staff resources. It's a complex concept in comparison to traditional top-down frameworks that are sometimes found in the private and public sectors.

> As we look ahead into the next century, leaders will be those who empower others.
>
> Bill Gates

The concept of shared leadership is explored in research conducted by Leslie Crutchfield and Heather McLeod Grant. In *Forces for Good: The Six Practices of High-Impact Nonprofits,* their research indicates that wise chief executives, "recognize that they must share power if they are to unleash and magnify the potential of their organizations. They learn to let go to have greater impact."[20]

For a select few executive directors, the ability to share leadership and empower others is an innate gift. For the majority, it is a philosophy to be learned, practiced and supported by implementing helpful tools. Passionate leaders often insist on providing final approval and struggle to let go of authority because they want everyone in their organization to do a great job and provide a quality product. They know they can count on themselves to deliver every time. It's not as easy to count on someone else to do the same. Not only does this create a bottleneck for the organization, it also leads to burnout for the executive director. There are several tools and techniques available to help you let others wow you by creating top-notch outcomes.

Central to this effort is to make sure you have the right team in place, whether it's staff, the board, or other volunteers. Next, you must clearly define your expectations and requirements, and then create feedback mechanisms that hold people accountable for results so they are appropriately rewarded or re-directed.

Hiring the Right Staff

Let's begin by exploring ways to ensure you have the right staff in place. In the nonprofit community, anyone you hire should first and foremost demonstrate passion for the mission; the *"what"* of the organization. The most talented person or skilled executive won't be the right fit if his/her passion lies elsewhere. That's not to say the *"who"* isn't important. A person you hire for ANY job must possess a complement of skills that they will contribute toward your organization's success. Hiring the right people will both increase productivity and decrease costs associated with turnover. Hiring wisely is a worthwhile investment of time, energy, and resources.

WRONG ANSWER!

I was part of a team that was looking to hire a leader. One of the key attributes we were looking for was a candidate's ability to acknowledge mistakes and view them as learning opportunities. This was important because the organization's prevailing culture was that people were afraid to experiment or take risks. Unsuccessful ventures and/or mistakes were frowned upon, and people were punished or ridiculed. The organization wanted to shift the culture to encourage experimentation and creativity and instill a belief that mistakes are an opportunity to learn. They decided to bring in new leaders who could help with the change.

We asked a candidate to describe a time he had made a mistake and explain the situation, what role he had played, and the result. He proceeded to describe a time he had made the mistake of letting his wife choose pavers for his home's front walkway. He thought he could trust her to pick a style that would complement the house and yard. The result, he said, was that the front walkway looked terrible. But to keep peace in the house, he never told his wife how much he hated it. Not only did this fellow pick a bad example - he saw it more of a mistake his wife made, not him, and wanted to lay the blame at her feet as well - he thought by not discussing his opinion of the outcome he was acting as a good leader. Needless to say, he wasn't a good fit for the organization and he wasn't asked back for a second interview.

Hiring Steps to Follow

Step 1:

The first step in making sure you have the right team in place is to clearly articulate skills and attributes necessary for each particular job title. You can accomplish this by developing a job description for every position in the organization. This becomes the foundation for hiring as well as outlining performance expectations. Any time a position becomes vacant, you should reassess the job description. Decide how to structure it to most effectively contribute to the success of the organization. It's possible the job is no longer relevant or necessary. Make sure the job description complies with requisite employment laws. A completed example of an Employee Job Description can be found in the Tools Section at the end of this chapter. For a blank template go to page 176. For a downloadable version go to www.LeadforGood.org.

Step 2:

After clarifying the most important elements of the position, create a selection grid that highlights the key job attributes. This will help objectify the process, keeping you and others focused on the necessary skills and behaviors. A completed example of a Position Selection Grid can be found in the Tools Section at the end of this chapter. For a blank template go to page 193. For a downloadable version go to www.LeadforGood.org.

Step 3:

Once you are clear on the most important skills and attributes for the job, create questions that help you determine whether a candidate fits your criteria. One of the best ways to identify whether a person is a successful candidate is to ask questions that reveal how a person has behaved in the past. Called a "Behavioral Interview," the answers to these types of questions are generally a good indicator of a person's future behavior. Asking behavioral questions is different than asking situational questions. Situational questions query a candidate about how she/he would handle a specific set of circumstances, e.g. "How would you handle a difficult co-worker?" An example of a behavioral question that elicits a more honest, non-rehearsed answer, is "Tell me about a time you had to deal with a difficult co-worker. What was the situation? What did you do about it? And, what was the result?"

Behavioral questions are three-pronged:

1. Ask the candidate to share a specific experience tied to the attribute you are trying to measure. For example, "Tell me about a time you participated in an effective collaboration. What was the situation?"
2. Ask the person to then explain his/her role and/or involvement in the situation. For example, "What role did you play in the collaboration?"
3. Ask the person about the outcome of the situation. For example, "What was the result of the collaboration?"

A copy of Behavioral Interview Question Options can be found on page 139. For a downloadable version go to www.LeadforGood.org.

Step 4:

Use social media to advertise job openings. The more specific you are regarding the type of work, position requirements, and benefits offered, the more likely qualified candidates will apply. Review resumes and applications to select candidates who appear to have most of the skills and meet all the minimum requirements.

Step 5:

Assign someone to conduct initial telephone interviews consisting of five to six questions to screen applicants and determine whether they are strong enough to be brought in for an interview. Telephone Interview Screening Question Options can be found on page 201. For a downloadable version go to www.LeadforGood.org.

Step 6:

Bring in the top three to six candidates for interviews by a small team. Team members should include the supervisor of the position, one or two peers of the position, and, if applicable, one or two people who will report to the position. Make every effort to help candidates feel comfortable and relaxed. This includes a pre-tour of the facility, introducing them to people in the organization, explaining the interview process, and offering water during the interview. Team members should alternate asking questions, with the option to ask a follow-up question. The interview should last about one hour and should consist of no more than eight to 10 questions. You also want to give candidates a chance to ask questions at the end of the interview.

Step 7:

Leave at least 30 minutes between interviews to conduct a debriefing session for each candidate. After a candidate leaves, each interviewer completes the selection grid for that person. Then, a volunteer from the group facilitates a conversation to reach consensus on a team rating for each of the criterion on the selection grid. Comparing results of all candidates should help determine who is the best fit for the position.

Building a Strong Board

Just as building a great staff is important to an organization, so is cultivating a strong board of directors. Having a capable board translates into more connections for resource development, better direction-setting and decision-making, and strong commitment to the implementation of sound business practices. Recruiting effective board members is similar to selecting candidates to fill an employee position. Create a job description so potential board members are clear about expectations. A completed example of a Board Member Job Description can be found in the Tools Section at the end of this chapter. For a blank template go to page 143. For a downloadable version go to www.LeadforGood.org.

According to Richard T. Ingram's *"Ten Basic Responsibilities of Nonprofit Boards,"* the basic roles and responsibilities of an effective board are to:

1. Determine the organization's mission and purpose.
2. Select the Chief Executive.
3. Support the Chief Executive and assess his or her performance.
4. Ensure effective organizational planning.
5. Ensure adequate resources.
6. Manage resources effectively.
7. Determine, monitor, and strengthen the organization's program and services.
8. Enhance the organization's public image.
9. Ensure legal and ethical behavior and maintain accountability.
10. Recruit and orient new board members and assess board performance.[21]

A copy of the *"Ten Basic Responsibilities of Nonprofit Boards"* can be found on page 202. For a downloadable version go to www.LeadforGood.org.

Base your selection on the board's needs. If you have specific gaps, for example you need an attorney to help with legal matters, focus your recruitment efforts on finding someone with that skill. Recruit with the future in mind, resisting temptation to consider current needs solely. Instead, position board membership to move your organization to the next level. Consider, for example, whether a candidate has what it takes to eventually step into the board chair role. Tie your recruitment efforts to the strategic initiatives the organization is undertaking. In other words, if building infrastructure is an important part of your strategic plan, then recruit someone who has expertise in that area. A completed example of a Board Recruitment Matrix can be found in the Tools Section at the end of this chapter. For a blank template go to page 144. For a downloadable version go to www.LeadforGood.org.

Another tool to support your board recruitment efforts is an application. It gives insight into candidates' skills, abilities and attributes, as well as an indication of their commitment to delivering on board member expectations. A blank template of a Board of Directors Application can be found on page 140. For a downloadable version go to www.LeadforGood.org.

Recruiting Other Impactful Volunteers

To make sure you are surrounded by effective volunteers, beyond those serving on the board, and create the right environment for sharing leadership, be sure the organization invests time and energy into the volunteer recruitment process. A potential gold mine of talent is available as professionals in the private sector consider retirement and encore engagements. As these baby boomers retire, many are looking for opportunities to continue to contribute and are seeking meaningful work. In some cases, they might even want to pursue employment opportunities.

An historical shift in the desires of volunteers requires those in the nonprofit community to re-think opportunities and processes for engaging them. Gone are the days when retirees were content doing unskilled, repetitive work. They seek opportunities to bring their expertise to an organization and truly make a difference. An excellent resource is the Coming of Age website (www.comingofage.org), which will help you consider how to integrate these potentially high-impact volunteers into your organization.

Another available pool of volunteers is the Generation Y (also known as Millennials) population. Born between 1981 and 1999, this group is uniquely committed to giving back to the community. Creating fun, impactful opportunities to attract young people to your cause could result in many new high-energy, effective volunteers.

Understanding the skills and aspirations of potential volunteers will help ensure the right individuals are selected for the best possible fit. Keep in mind that happy volunteers become valuable donors! A blank template of a Volunteer Application can be found on page 205. For a downloadable version go to www.LeadforGood.org.

Empowering Others by Delegating Authority

Effective leaders share authority and empower others to advance the organization's mission and vision. Delegate authority to as many as you can. Encourage them to tap their creativity and take responsibility for developing ideas and delivering products and services. Doing so gives others an opportunity to gain experience and improve their skills. As more people participate, you will begin to see growth in your organization's impact on the community you serve. Learning to transfer the responsibility for how work is completed to others will allow you to operate more strategically.

Micromanagers see only narrow views. They create bottlenecks, stifle creativity and slow work because their "permission" is required at every turn. Shifting your energy to that of a leader with broad oversight builds trust while empowering others to get work done. A positive consequence of this shift in approach is often improved morale and reduced turnover. Allowing others to unleash their creativity leads to better end products and a more highly skilled workforce. It also frees you to pursue bigger picture activities and builds in a bit of much needed down-time that reduces your potential for burnout.

This said, it's not easy sharing power and allowing staff or volunteers to take leadership roles. You are likely to feel increased risk as you loosen your grip on control. Putting mechanisms in place to avoid missteps, embarrassments, and unexpected developments greatly reduces the likelihood of unwelcomed outcomes.

Establishing Degrees of Decision-Making

Letting go doesn't mean taking a hands-off approach. After all, anything can happen if no safeguards are in place to filter activities and materials your organization produces. One such protection is the Decision-Making Levels of Authority scale that you can use to determine the level of autonomy an individual is given related to a specific project.

Decision-Making Levels of Authority

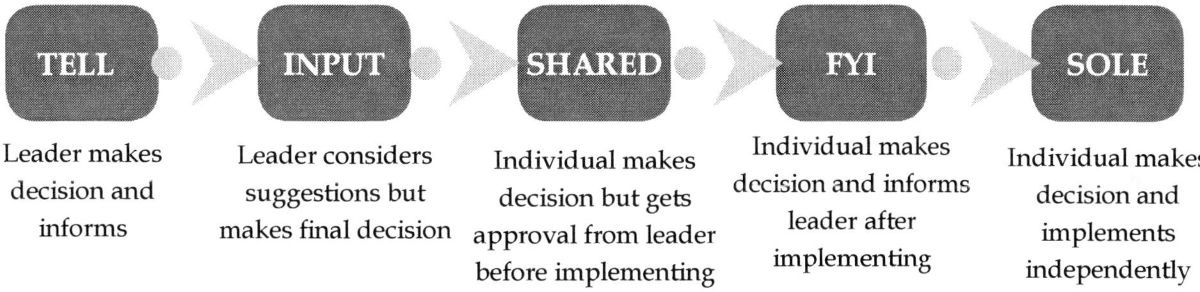

Recognizing the line between over-and under-orchestrating the delivery of work is easier when this communication process is in place and progress is discussed regularly in one-on-one meetings. Knowing when to step back and when to lean in varies based on such things as the complexity of the task, the experience level and competence of the person in charge of completing it, and whether the project is high risk and/or high profile. The scale is presented here as an illustration to help you visualize how the levels vary.

Using a common language to mutually agree on the level of autonomy at the beginning of a project, or as part of the performance management process, goes a long way in building trust and mutual respect between a leader and those with whom she/he works. A copy of the Decision-Making Levels of Authority can be found on page 175. For a downloadable version go to www.LeadforGood.org.

Clarifying Expectations – Performance Management

To ensure individuals clearly understand what is expected of them and their level of authority on any given project, adopt a performance management system tied to the strategic plan for your organization. This serves three primary purposes:

1. It helps individuals understand how their work directly contributes to the organization's vision, mission, and success.
2. It ensures alignment of work with attaining the overall goals outlined in the plan.
3. It creates a mechanism for feedback and accountability.

The process for creating a performance management system is outlined below. This approach is effective with staff and other key volunteers. The end result of following these steps is an annual performance review for each person in your organization. To clarify the process and demonstrate how the tools relate to one another, all the performance management examples at the end of the chapter refer to a CEO Administrative Assistant.

1. Make sure each person's job description is updated to accurately reflect work being done. Ask the person who is doing the job to create a draft and then revise it together. A completed example of an Employee Job Description can be found in the Tools Section at the end of this chapter. For a blank template go to page 176. For a downloadable version go to www.LeadforGood.org.
2. Identify key accountabilities (should be three to five) for the job and then decide what important activities support each of the accountabilities. Partner with the individual to decide what measure(s) are appropriate to determine success. Completed examples of Performance Review Accountability Worksheets 1 & 2 can be found in the Tools Section at the end of this chapter. For blank templates go to pages 188 and 189. For downloadable versions go to www.LeadforGood.org.
3. Complete a performance review accountability workform based on the accountabilities before the start of the review period so the individual is clear on expectations from the start. A completed example of the Performance Review Accountability Workform can be found in the Tools Section at the end of this chapter. For a blank template go to page 190. For a downloadable version go to www.LeadforGood.org.
4. Establish an appropriate decision-making level of authority for each activity. That way, both you and the individual will be clear on what kind of check-in is required

for each of the defined activities. This clarity is helpful in avoiding conflict going forward. A copy of the Decision-Making Levels of Authority can be found on page 175. For a downloadable version go to www.LeadforGood.org.

5. Complete the performance review based on the employee's delivery on agreed-upon accountabilities and measures. The more specific examples and observations included, the more valuable and impactful the review. A completed example of a Performance Review can be found in the Tools Section at the end of this chapter. For a blank template go to page 185. For a downloadable version go to www.LeadforGood.org.

The Take Away

The ability to share leadership is another crucial competency needed to be an effective leader. Working in the nonprofit sector requires leaders to partner with others to co-create and collaborate in an arena where multiple stakeholders and limited resources are standard.

It is not easy to relinquish control of your organization's activities while still being held accountable. It is a skill acquired through practice. The tools provided in this chapter are designed to foster organization-wide confidence that others will use to appropriately unleash their creativity and deliver what's needed for the organization to make progress and achieve its goals. Keys to success are hiring strong staff, recruiting savvy board members, filling key volunteer roles with self-directed go-getters, and clarifying expectations.

TOOLS ● STEP 5
SHARE LEADERSHIP

EXAMPLE
EMPLOYEE JOB DESCRIPTION

JOB TITLE CEO Administrative Assistant EFFECTIVE DATE: 4/12/10
EEO CODE: 5 REVISION DATE: 11/2/14
REPORTS TO: CEO FSLA: Non-exempt

PURPOSE:

The purpose of this position is to provide administrative support to the CEO. In addition, the position provides administrative services, communications, meeting planning, and back-up telephone support to the organization as needed.

PRINCIPLE ACCOUNTABILITIES:

- Manage the CEO's schedule
- Manage CEO phone calls and redirect as needed
- Prepare materials, reports and special projects as requested
- Sort and deliver mail
- Take and distribute manager, staff, and board meeting minutes
- Arrange for travel for the CEO
- Manage the expense-reporting process for the CEO
- Communicate information to staff as requested
- Provide back-up support on telephone
- Prepare board meeting notices, agendas and support materials for meetings
- Distribute monthly board packets
- Plan meetings and staff events

QUALIFICATIONS:

- High School Diploma or Equivalent required
- 5-7 years of administrative experience required
- Ability to stay calm under pressure required
- Must be able to prioritize work based on agreed-upon parameters
- Ability to multitask a must
- Strong writing and oral communication skills required
- Ability to speak Spanish preferred
- 1-3 years event planning experience required
- Strong customer-service skills required
- Excellent typing skills preferred
- Microsoft Office product experience preferred

CRITICAL FUNCTIONS:

- Use a Telephone
- Use a computer
- Communicate with others verbally and in writing

EXAMPLE
POSITION SELECTION GRID

List key criteria for the specific job

Use a multiplier for the most important

JOB CANDIDATES	PASSION AROUND ISSUE OF DOMESTIC VIOLENCE X2	KNOWLEDGE OF HUMAN RESOURCE LAWS X3	EFFECTIVE COLLABORATOR X2	HAS POTENTIAL FOR GROWTH AND PROMOTION	EFFECTIVE ORAL AND WRITTEN COMMUNICATOR	THINKS STRATEGICALLY	EXPERIENCE ADDRESSING CONFLICT EFFECTIVELY X2	DEMONSTRATES COMMITMENT TO BOTH INTERNAL AND EXTERNAL CUSTOMERS	TOTAL
B. Jones	4 X 2 = 8	3 x 3 = 9	4 X 2 = 8	**4**	**4**	**3**	3 x 2 = 6	4	**46**
E. Bibbs	4 X 2 = 8	3 x 3 = 9	5 x 2 = 10	**5**	**4**	**4**	4 X 2 = 8	5	**53**
T. Randall	3 x 2 = 6	3 x 3 = 9	2 x 2 = 4	**3**	**3**	**3**	4 X 2 = 8	3	**39**
P. Simms	5 x 2 = 10	3 x 3 = 9	5 x 2 = 10	**3**	**3**	**4**	4 X 2 = 8	5	**51**

Use a scale of 0-5 to rate how well the job candidate under consideration fits each of the criterion. If not sure about a specific criterion, give it a "3." If a criterion is especially important, a multiplier of 2 or 3 may be added.

In this example, the best candidate is E. Bibbs with a score of 53. A close second is P. Simms with a score of 51.

EXAMPLE
BOARD MEMBER JOB DESCRIPTION

JOB TITLE: Board Member EFFECTIVE DATE: 8/11

REPORTS TO: Board Chairperson REVISION DATE: 6/14

PURPOSE:

Supports the process for identifying and stewarding the organization's mission and purpose. In addition, this position aids with the selection and support of the chief executive, facilitates the availability of adequate resources, shares fiduciary responsibility for the organization, and ensures legal and ethical accountability.

PRINCIPLE ACCOUNTABILITIES:

- Be informed about and promote the organization's mission, services, and programs
- Prepare for meetings by reviewing materials in advance
- Fully participate in all board and committee meetings and functions
- Fully participate on committees or task forces
- Hold self and others accountable for delivering on commitments
- Make a personal financial contribution to the organization and support generating contributions from other sources
- Be familiar with and follow all policies, including conflict of interest and confidentiality
- Direct all inquiries and requests to the chief executive
- Proactively assist the board in carrying out its fiduciary responsibilities by reviewing the organization's monthly and annual financial statements and sharing any concerns or suggestions regarding the financial health of the organization

QUALIFICATIONS:

- Believes in the primary mission and purpose of the organization
- Creative problem-solver who listens and is receptive to new and different ideas
- Able to commit time and resources to support the organization
- Willing to participate in cultivating and soliciting funds for the organization
- Demonstrates honesty and integrity in carrying out duties as a board member
- Consistently delivers on commitments made to the organization

EXAMPLE
BOARD RECRUITMENT MATRIX

To use, start by putting the initials of each current board member into the appropriate box, based on his/her attributes. It will give you an indication where you have gaps in order to appropriately recruit new board members. The matrix is set up to accommodate 18 board members who serve three year terms. The number of columns and number of "classes" should be changed to match the number of board members and term lengths outlined in the organization's by-laws.

In the example, Andrew Ford (AF), Tina Smith (TS), Lauren Eldridge (LE), and Joseph Johnson (JJ) are current board members. There are gaps in ethnicity - no Native-American or Asian-American representatives; constituency – no government or community representatives; and skills – no fundraising or planning representatives. These would be areas to focus on for board recruitment.

	CLASS OF 2018						CLASS OF 2019						CLASS OF 2020					
GROUP:																		
Female	TS												LE					
Male							AF	JJ										
20-35							AF						LE					
36-55	TS																	
Over 55								JJ										
Caucasian	TS						AF											
African American													LE					
Latino								JJ										
Native American																		
Asian-American																		
Other:																		

BOARD RECRUITMENT MATRIX - Page 2

	CLASS OF 2018						CLASS OF 2019						CLASS OF 2020					
DEMOGRAPHIC:																		
Inner City							AF	JJ										
Suburban													LE					
Rural	TS																	
Other:																		
CONSTITUENCY:																		
Business	TS							JJ					LE					
Government																		
Program/Product User							AF											
Community																		
Other:																		
SKILLS:																		
Fundraising																		
Public Relations	TS																	
Planning																		
Financial								JJ										
Human Resources													LE					
Legal													LE					
Program/Product Expertise							AF											
Technology	TS																	
Other:																		

EXAMPLE

PERFORMANCE REVIEW ACCOUNTABILITY WORKSHEET 1

Name: CEO Administrative Assistant

Accountability 1: Support CEO

Action Steps:

- Manage CEO's schedule
- Manage CEO phone calls and redirect as appropriate
- Prepare materials, reports and special projects as requested
- Sort/deliver mail
- Take manager and staff meeting minutes
- Arrange trips as requested and process expenses

Accountability 2: Support the Organization

Action Steps:

- Organize/provide admin support (prepare materials, order supplies, assist with projects)
- Communicate – keep team informed of important/key org info
- Provide back-up for phone overflow, visitors, etc.

Accountability 3: Prepare Board and Committee Communications

Action Steps:

- Prepare meeting notices, agendas and support materials
- Take meeting minutes
- Distribute monthly board packets
- Keep files for each committee and board correspondence

Accountability 4: Plan Staff Meetings/Celebrations

Action Steps:

- Arrange for convenient locations for meetings/gatherings
- Ensure all materials, equipment and refreshments are provided as requested
- Coordinate staff picnic and holiday party

EXAMPLE

PERFORMANCE REVIEW ACCOUNTABILITY WORKSHEET 2

Name: CEO Administrative Assistant

Accountability 1: Support CEO

Action Steps:	Measurements:
Manage CEO's schedule	Update 3 times per week (M,W,F) – call voicemail w/last minute changes
Manage CEO phone calls and redirect as appropriate	Calls are answered by third ring
Prepare materials, regular reports and special projects as requested	CEO perceives materials prepared in a timely manner
Sort/deliver mail	Deliver daily and pick up CEO outbox materials twice daily
Take manager and staff meeting minutes	Completed and distributed to staff within 2 days
Arrange trips as requested an process expenses	CEO perceives gets info in timely manner and expenses processed at least once per month

Accountability 2: Support the Organization

Action Steps:	Measurements:
Organize/provide admin support (prepare materials, order supplies, assist with projects)	Materials/projects prepared by requested deadline as measured by survey feedback
Communicate – keep team informed of important/key organizational information	Team receives info with time to act upon it (80% favorable on survey on timeliness of communications)
Provide backup for phone overflow, visitors, etc.	Team is satisfied with teamwork provided (80% favorable on survey on teamwork)

Accountability 3: Prepare Board and Committee Communications

Action Steps:	Measurements:
Prepare meeting notices, agendas and support materials	Materials are prepared three days prior to the scheduled meeting
Take meeting minutes	Minutes are sent to CEO for review and revisions within two days and distributed within five days
Distribute monthly board packets	Board packet sent one week prior to board meeting
Keep files for each committee and board correspondence	Files are updated weekly

Accountability 4: Plan Staff Meetings/Celebrations

Action Steps:	Measurements:
Arrange for convenient locations for meetings/gatherings	Locations secured within one week of request and meet budget requirements
Ensure all materials, equipment and refreshments are provided as requested	80% of those who request meeting support indicate they are satisfied with support provided
Coordinate staff picnic and holiday party	Functions don't exceed budget

EXAMPLE
PERFORMANCE REVIEW ACCOUNTABILITY WORKFORM

ACCOUNTABILITY	RESULTS EXPECTED	ACTIONS STEPS	STANDARD/ MEASUREMENT	LEVEL OF AUTHORITY	ASSISTANCE REQUIRED
Your three to five major responsibilities. The big ones- the reason the job exists. Action oriented.	**What you hope to accomplish – the reason why you do the accountability.**	**How you hope to achieve the expected results.**	**How you measure each action step.**	**What level of authority is granted to accomplish each action step.**	**From whom do you need help?**
1. SUPPORT CEO	• CEO is freed to focus on strategic issues	• Manage CEO's schedule	• Update 3 times per week (M, W, F) – call voicemail w/last minute changes	FYI	
	• Internal customer needs are better served	• Manage CEO phone calls and redirect as needed	• Calls are answered by third ring	Sole	
		• Prepare regular reports and special projects as requested	• CEO perceives materials prepared in a timely manner	Sole/Shared	CEO
		• Sort/deliver mail	• Deliver and pick up CEO outbox materials twice daily	Sole	
		• Take manager and staff meeting minutes	• Completed and distributed to staff within 2 days	FYI	
		• Arrange trips as requested and process expenses	• CEO satisfied and expenses processed at least once per month	FYI	Accounting Department
2. SUPPORT THE ORGANIZATION	• Individuals are free to focus on their work plans	• Organize/provide admin support (prep materials, order supplies, assist with projects)	• Materials/projects prepared by requested deadline as measured by survey feedback	Sole	
	• Internal customer needs are better served	• Communicate – keep team informed of important/key information	• Team receives info with time to act upon it (80% favorable on survey on timeliness of communications)	Shared	
		• Provide backup for phone overflow, visitors, etc.	• Team is satisfied (80% favorable on survey on teamwork)	Sole	

PERFORMANCE REVIEW ACCOUNTABILITY WORKFORM - Page 2

ACCOUNTABILITY	RESULTS EXPECTED	ACTIONS STEPS	STANDARD/ MEASUREMENT	LEVEL OF AUTHORITY	ASSISTANCE REQUIRED
Your three to five major responsibilities. The big ones- the reason the job exists. Action oriented.	**What you hope to accomplish – the reason why you do the accountability.**	**How you hope to achieve the expected results.**	**How you measure each action step.**	**What level of authority is granted to accomplish each action step.**	**From whom do you need help?**
3. PREPARE BOARD AND COMMITTEE COMMUNICATIONS	• Ensure board members are informed about important issues facing the organization	• Prepare meeting notices, agendas and support materials	• Materials are prepared eight days prior to the scheduled meeting	Shared	Person holding meeting
		• Take meeting minutes	• Minutes are sent to CEO for review in two days and distributed within five days	Shared	CEO
	• Assist in maximizing the productivity of board meetings	• Distribute monthly board packets	• Board packet sent one week prior to board meeting	Shared	Contributors to board packet
		• Keep files for each committee and board correspondence	• Files are updated weekly	Sole	
4. PLAN STAFF MEETINGS/ CELEBRATIONS	• Improve communications within the organization	• Arrange for convenient locations for meetings/gatherings	• Locations secured within one week of request and meet budget requirements	Shared	Staff meeting requestor
		• Ensure all materials, equipment and refreshments are provided as requested	• 80% of those who request meeting support indicate they are satisfied with support provided	Shared	Staff meeting requestor
	• Employees feel valued	• Coordinate staff picnic and holiday party	• Functions don't exceed budget	Shared	CEO and/or CFO

EXAMPLE
PERFORMANCE REVIEW

Employee Name: Donna Harris **Review Date:** June 12
Position Title: CEO Administrative Assistant **Name of Reviewer:** Sally

Accountability Review

Summarize progress on meeting accountabilities during the review period, using employee input. The leader should complete a draft then meet with the employee to discuss and agree on the final content.

With Distinction - 1 | Successful - 2 | Needs Improvement - 3

ACCOUNTABILITIES/ ACTION STEPS	ACHIEVEMENTS/ OPPORTUNITIES *(COMPARE ACCOUNTABILITY MEASURE TO ACTUAL PERFORMANCE)*	SELF/LEADER OBSERVATIONS *(USE SPECIFIC EXAMPLES)*
Support CEO:		
• Manage CEO's schedule	Check-in 3x weekly Rating: 2	Donna has done a solid job supporting me over the last 12 months. While she had a learning curve because she was new to the position, we had regular check-ins to make sure my schedule was in sync and I was aware of all meetings and how I needed to prepare for each.
• Manage CEO phone calls and redirect as appropriate	Calls answered properly Rating: 2	
• Prepare materials, regular reports and special projects as requested	Materials well-prepared Rating: 2	Donna did a terrific job in August when she supported our big annual meeting with key stakeholders. I had several comments from board members that she was warm and helpful and made sure all the materials were error-free and ready as needed.
• Sort/deliver mail	Mail handled 2x daily Rating: 2	She regularly sorted and delivered the mail and made sure all phone calls were answered in a timely manner. The only exception is when she took vacation back in November. She neglected to arrange for anyone to cover her mail or phone duties during her absence. She needed to put a plan in place because our level of service suffered until we figured out a way to get things covered. She was very open to having a conversation about the issue, and it has not recurred since that time.

PERFORMANCE REVIEW - Page 2

ACCOUNTABILITIES/ ACTION STEPS	ACHIEVEMENTS/ OPPORTUNITIES *(COMPARE ACCOUNTABILITY MEASURE TO ACTUAL PERFORMANCE)*	SELF/LEADER OBSERVATIONS *(USE SPECIFIC EXAMPLES)*
Support CEO Continued:		
• Take manager and staff meeting minutes	Complete/distribute within 2 days Rating: 3	As for meeting minutes, Donna had a difficult time getting them distributed within 48 hours. She often struggled to take accurate notes and regularly had to check with others to verify what she thought she heard. In addition, much like the calls and mail issue, no arrangements were made by her to cover this responsibility while she was on vacation. Again, we spoke about it and agreed it was an oversight on her part and was an expected part of her job.
• Arrange trips as requested and process expenses	Plan trips and handle expenses Rating: 1	
	OVERALL RATING for Supports CEO: 2 (Average of all ratings for this accountability.)	Donna is a great travel planner. The best I've ever seen! She saved many hundreds of dollars because she looked for deals every time I had to travel. She even rebooked one of my flights because the price dropped. She also submitted the receipts efficiently and in a timely manner.

PERFORMANCE REVIEW - Page 3

ACCOUNTABILITIES/ ACTION STEPS	ACHIEVEMENTS/ OPPORTUNITIES *(COMPARE ACCOUNTABILITY MEASURE TO ACTUAL PERFORMANCE)*	SELF/LEADER OBSERVATIONS *(USE SPECIFIC EXAMPLES)*
Support the Organization:		
• Organize/provide admin support (prepare materials, order supplies, assist with projects)	Materials/projects prepared by requested deadline as measured by survey feedback Rating: 2	A survey conducted among internal customers indicated Donna has done a great job getting to know everyone and 82% said she is an active contributor to the team. One respondent indicated Donna had volunteered to cover the front lobby so that she could attend her child's recital and another said Donna had rolled up her sleeves and helped put together packets for a training session being handled by one of the program coordinators.
• Communicate – keep team informed of important/key organizational information	Team receives info with time to act upon it (80% favorable on survey on timeliness of communications) Rating: 2	84% of all respondents indicated Donna is a good communicator and distributes information in a timely fashion. She also delivers materials for projects in a timely manner without the need to ask over and over.
• Provide backup for phone overflow, visitors, etc.	Team is satisfied with teamwork provided (80% favorable on survey on teamwork) Rating: 1 **OVERALL RATING for Support the Organization: 2**	Overall, Donna's teamwork rating among internal customers was 87% favorable. This is an excellent score especially since Donna was new to the organization and had a lot to learn.

PERFORMANCE REVIEW - Page 4

ACCOUNTABILITIES/ ACTION STEPS	ACHIEVEMENTS/ OPPORTUNITIES *(COMPARE ACCOUNTABILITY MEASURE TO ACTUAL PERFORMANCE)*	SELF/LEADER OBSERVATIONS *(USE SPECIFIC EXAMPLES)*
Prepare Board and Committee Communications:		
• Prepare meeting notices, agendas and support materials	Materials are prepared eight days prior to the scheduled meeting Rating: 2	Donna worked hard to coordinate the preparation and deliver of materials out to the board and committees prior to meeting dates. Generally, if she didn't make the eight day in advance timeframe, it was more due to not getting the materials in time from others rather than any issue on her end. I know I was guilty of not delivering required information in a timely manner at least four times during the review period.
• Take meeting minutes	Minutes are sent to CEO for review and revisions within two days and distributed within five days Rating: 3	As for meeting minutes, however, Donna really struggled to get them done within the 48-hour window. This has been an on-going issue, whether the minutes are for board meetings or staff meetings. She missed the 48-hour timeframe 60% of the time for the delivery of board meeting minutes to me for review.
• Distribute monthly board packets	Board packet sent one week prior to board meeting Rating: 2	
• Keep files for each committee and board correspondence	Files are updated weekly Rating: 3	Donna also struggled with keeping up with the filing. After discussing it, it is clear this is not a task she enjoys, so we will work together to find a resource (volunteer or intern) to help with it. This may also give her a chance to practice her supervisory skills.
	OVERALL RATING for Prepare Board and Committee Communications: 2	

PERFORMANCE REVIEW - Page 5

ACCOUNTABILITIES/ ACTION STEPS	ACHIEVEMENTS/ OPPORTUNITIES *(COMPARE ACCOUNTABILITY MEASURE TO ACTUAL PERFORMANCE)*	SELF/LEADER OBSERVATIONS *(USE SPECIFIC EXAMPLES)*
Plan Staff Meetings/Celebrations:		
• Arrange for convenient locations for meetings/gatherings	Locations secured within one week of request and meet budget requirements Rating: 1	Planning and executing events is definitely a strong skill for Donna. Feedback from every single internal customers (100%) indicated she did a terrific job planning and executing meetings and celebrations. Of the nine meetings/events she planned, Donna came in below budget on seven of them. And, she was on budget for the other two....none were over budget!
• Ensure all materials, equipment and refreshments are provided as requested	80% of those who request meeting support indicate they are satisfied with support provided Rating: 1	
• Coordinate staff picnic and holiday party	Functions don't exceed budget Rating: 1 **OVERALL RATING for Plan Staff Meetings/Celebrations: 1**	

OVERALL RATING: 2

PERFORMANCE REVIEW - Page 6

What performance strengths has the employee exhibited during the review period? Be sure to note examples of work well done, special projects completed, new responsibilities taken on and/or any other key accomplishments.
Donna has clearly demonstrated she is an excellent travel and event planner. Every gathering was beautifully planned and executed. Further, she is an excellent steward of our nonprofit's limited resources. She exceeded all expectations regarding staying on or below budget. Another strength is the speed in which she integrated into the organization and her position as CEO Administrative Assistant. Feedback from both staff and volunteers is that she is warm, helpful, and truly cares about the organization and the work we do.
What performance weaknesses or difficulties did the employee exhibit during the review period?
Donna needs to work on anticipating needs and identifying problems before they happen, as evidenced by the lack of planning for her vacation. We are a small nonprofit organization, and we are very dependent on her to make sure things run smoothly, even in her absence. In addition, she needs to improve on her minute-taking capabilities. Keeping accurate records of proceedings and having a ready reference in a timely manner are critical for the efficient operation of the organization.

JOB RELATED OBJECTIVES

Indicate below the objectives to be met during the next review period and recommendations for meeting these objectives. Be sure to cover performance areas in which the employee needs improvement.

OBJECTIVES	RECOMMENDATIONS
Leverage meeting/event skills to support fundraising efforts.	Meet with the fundraising director to determine how best to partner with her to support fundraising events. Adjust your accountabilities to reduce other responsibilities to support having the time to focus on events.
Offload filing duties to another resource.	Work with the volunteer coordinator to identify someone to handle this task going forward. This person would report to you and you would manage the process to ensure it was completed correctly and in a timely manner.
Improve delivery on minutes for staff and board meetings.	Purchase Dragon Software to experiment with using it for recording/capturing meeting minutes. Or, consider recording minutes and transcribing them at a later time.

CHAPTER SIX • STEP 6
BUILD STRONG COMMUNITY RELATIONSHIPS

Watchwords for the nonprofit sector these days are "collaboration" and "collective impact." With money scarce, organizations that share and leverage resources are the ones funders like to support. Increasing your organization's potential to receive contributions and grants means more opportunity to make a difference. A shift in thinking is occurring that frames nonprofit work as strengths-based rather than needs-based. Organizations are focusing on the assets they have, and how they might leverage those existing strengths to better serve constituents. It's an abundance mentality: The belief that helping other organizations by sharing resources and working together ultimately helps all organizations better serve their missions.

John P. Kretzmann and John L. McKnight founded the Asset Based Community Development Institute (ABCD) at Northwestern University to support the movement that considers local assets of residents, associations and institutions as primary building blocks of sustainable community development. For more information about ABCD and the Institute, go to www.abcdinstitute.org.

> "True community requires commitment and openness. It is a willingness to extend yourself to encounter and know the other.
>
> David Spangler"

Key principles and assumptions of Asset Based Community Development include the following:

1. Everyone has gifts.
2. Relationships build a community.
3. Citizens at the center can engage the wider community.

4. Leaders involve others as active members of the community.
5. People care about something.
6. Motivation to act must be identified.
7. Listening conversations are key.
8. Ask, ask, ask others to join.
9. Asking questions rather than giving answers invites stronger participation.
10. A citizen-centered "inside-out" organization is the key to community engagement.
11. Institutions have reached their limits in problem-solving.
12. Leaders of institutions can lead by "stepping back" thereby creating opportunity for citizenship, care and real democracy.[22]

Partnering Continuum

Partnering is a sliding scale of commitment. In their work, *Collaboration Handbook: Creating, Sustaining, and Enjoying the Journey,* Michael Winer and Karen Ray explain partnerships in terms of three levels.[23] The first, least intense level is **cooperation**. Cooperation involves shorter-term informal relationships that exist without a clearly defined mission, structure, or planning effort. Cooperative partners share information only about subjects at hand. Each organization retains authority and keeps resources separate to minimize risk.

Coordination, the second level, involves formalizing relationships and calls for building trust-based relationships and opening lines of communication between organizations. People involved in coordinated activities focus longer-term interactions around specific efforts or programs. While authority rests with individual organizations, risk increases as power, resources and success or failure is shared.

The third level is **collaboration**, a more intense form of working together involving a greater amount of time and trust. Winer and Ray describe it as "a more durable and pervasive relationship...Participants bring separate organizations into a new structure with full commitment to a common mission."[24] These relationships require comprehensive planning and well-defined communication channels that operate at all levels. Risk is increased because each partner contributes resources and its reputation. Partners pool or jointly secure resources, sharing results and rewards or losses.

In the last few years, a new model has emerged that substantially elevates both impact and risk to tackle large scale community issues such as homelessness and food insecurity.

Masterfully articulated by John Kania and Mark Kramer, it is called **collective impact**. This approach focuses on implementing cross-sector changes that require trust and shared leadership at the highest levels.[25] According to Jeff Edmondson, there are four key distinctions between collaboration and collective impact:

Collaboration		**Collective Impact**
Convene Around Programs/Initiatives	→	Work Together to Move Outcomes
Prove	→	Improve
Addition to What You Do	→	Is What You Do
Advocates for Ideas	→	Advocate for What Works[26]

For collective impact to work, the following five conditions must be met:

1. **Common Agenda:** All participants have a shared vision for change including a common understanding of the problem and a joint approach to solving it through agreed upon actions.
2. **Shared Measurement:** Collecting data and measuring results consistently across all participants ensure the efforts remain aligned and participants hold each other accountable.
3. **Mutually Reinforcing Activities:** Participant activities must be differentiated while still being coordinated through a mutually reinforcing plan of action.
4. **Continuous Communication:** Consistent and open communication is needed across the many players to build trust, assure mutual objectives, and create common motivation.
5. **Backbone Support:** Creating and managing collective impact requires a separate organization(s) with staff and a specific set of skills to serve as the backbone for the entire initiative and coordinate participating organizations and agencies.[27]

A copy of the Collective Impact Conditions Required can be found on page 165. For a downloadable version go to www.LeadforGood.org.

All options to partner have potential for garnering impactful results. However, from a leadership perspective, they become progressively more difficult to implement as interdependency intensifies. As work becomes increasingly intertwined, it often requires leaders to relinquish and share authority, trust the process, take a back seat, and serve in a support role. As discussed in the last chapter, this usually proves difficult for leaders who are accustomed to being in charge, charting direction, and single-handedly rallying people to a cause. Here are a few questions to ask yourself to get a sense of your level of readiness to be a collaborator.[28] The full Collaborability Assessment is available on page 164. For a downloadable version go to www.LeadforGood.org.

MINI ACTIVITY

ARE YOU COLLABORATIVE?

Please rate yourself on a scale of 1 to 5, 1 being needs development and 5 being very strong, on the following aspects of your collaborability.

1. Being challenged without taking it personally

1	2	3	4	5
Needs Development				Very Strong

2. Building on other people's ideas without fearing my idea will be diminished

1	2	3	4	5
Needs Development				Very Strong

3. Pausing to allow time for reflection & thinking

1	2	3	4	5
Needs Development				Very Strong

4. Presuming positive intentions of others during discussions

1	2	3	4	5
Needs Development				Very Strong

5. Being able to see failure as a contributor to innovation

1	2	3	4	5
Needs Development				Very Strong

Source: Debra Exner and Maddie Hunter, www.CollaborationPaysOff.com, 2008

Relinquishing authority and building strong, trusting relationships in the community are vitally important. Crutchfield and Grant capture the essence as they note, "...we have come to believe that sharing leadership has in fact enabled nonprofits to have more impact. Because they [high impact nonprofits] focus so much on influencing players outside their organizational boundaries, they need to manage hundreds of relationships and access many networks."[29]

Lessons learned from the Philadelphia Multiple Myeloma Networking Group (PMMNG) are applicable to any leader who is striving toward more collaborative relationships with outside partners.

1. **Collaborate widely** - Leaders at PMMNG sought support from organizations such as the International Management Foundation, The Wellness Community, the Leukemia and Lymphoma Society, and the Multiple Myeloma Research Foundation.

2. **Do what it takes to accomplish the vision** - Leaders at PMMNG decided to become an independent 501(c)3 when their size and vision grew. Then, a tragic loss of an important leader illustrated the need to create a shared leadership model that provided coverage and succession plans.

3. **Think big** - Today PMMNG is a highly collaborative 501(c)3 that serves as a regional network of support. The organization mentors other support groups, engages in fundraising for research and political advocacy, and has built dozens of relationships with organizations throughout the region. Currently, the group is viewed as a source for input on the development of clinical trials and scientific research agendas for some of its partners.[30]

LIFE and DEATH

When collaboration is successful, it can mean the difference between life and death. Take for example the Philadelphia Multiple Myeloma Networking Group (PMMNG). Like many nonprofit organizations, it had its start around a kitchen table. When Marilyn Alexander was diagnosed with a rare, potentially fatal illness in 1995, she and her twin sister Sharon Klein found few resources to guide them. Along with others, the cofounders of PMMNG created an organization for patients with myeloma that provides information, support, shared experiences and hope.

More than 15 years after diagnosis with an illness that has traditionally carried a short life expectancy, many of the original founders are still thriving and serving as a network that helps patients throughout the region. Everyone in the myeloma community takes great comfort in knowing that the network is strong and will continue to exist due to the collaborative efforts of so many people.

Strengths-Based Tools for Transforming and Exploring Partnerships

Making a transition from a cooperative partnership to one with collective impact is a multi-stepped process that should not be attempted all at once. It makes more sense to ease into working with other organizations by taking incremental steps. Tools have emerged during the last several years designed to explore and build partnerships in the social sector. Three of the most effective are Appreciative Inquiry, World Café, and Open Space Technology. Using one or all of these will help you get started in order to build enough "muscle" to support collaboration or collective impact.

Appreciative Inquiry

Innovator David Cooperrider originally developed the concept of appreciative inquiry pertaining to forging relationships among disparate groups. The approach has evolved over time and now has four phases: Discovery, Dream, Design and Delivery.[31] In the **Discovery Phase,** attention is paid to peak moments in the life of a partnership—when people have experienced the partnership relationship as most alive and effective. People will share stories about their accomplishments, strengths, and what elements they wish to carry forward in the future. As part of the process, participants working in pairs answer a series of questions. A copy of the Questions to Consider Asking During the Discovery Phase of Appreciative Inquiry can be found on page 196. For a downloadable version go to www.LeadforGood.org.

The **Dream Phase** is the second component of the 4-D model. During this phase, participants are challenged to use stories, data, and best practices surrounding their partnership experiences to think creatively about what the partnership might become. This exercise includes putting bold ideas into statements as if they have already been achieved. Called possibility propositions, these provocative statements are compelling precisely because they are based on successful partnerships that have already occurred.

Creating a work plan occurs in the **Design Phase** of the process. It's critical to align jointly-held visions and values and to reach consensus about what needs to happen to convert dreams into reality. The Strategic Planning Document tool presented in Chapter Three could prove helpful in clarifying details.

The **Delivery Phase** is the final phase of the 4-D model. Here, all parties involved agree to stay committed to continuously learning and to implementing adjustments along the way ensuring their shared vision remains vibrant. This involves remaining actively engaged in conversations about how things are going, and addressing issues that arise.[32]

World Café

Another good process for facilitating collaboration is the World Café model, which creates meaningful conversations and allows people to share thoughts and feelings in a comfortable environment. It gives participants an opportunity to listen to the perspectives of others and identify constructive possibilities as well as actively engage and be heard by others. A free reference guide is available courtesy of The World Café at www.theworldcafe.com. In it, an outline of how to host a world café is provided. Recommended guidelines include:

- **Clarifying purpose** happens by being intentional about why you are bringing people together and ensuring the right participants are invited to the conversation.

- **Creating hospitable space** considers how your invitation and physical set-up contribute to creating a comfortable environment. Suggestions include arranging multiple tables of four and covering the tables with butcher paper for doodling. Providing colorful water-based markers, pipe cleaners, and Play-Doh™ will give

WORLD CAFÉ IN ACTION

The Southwest Office of the Defenders of Wildlife recognized the need to do something different to engage the Tucson, Arizona community it serves. Realizing that facts, figures, and logical arguments were not enough to engage citizens effectively, the Wildlife Defenders did something different. They convened a group of artists and wildlife conservationists using the World Café approach to brainstorm ideas about how to engage citizens. Specifically, the organizers wanted participants to learn about the importance of the jaguar, the history of the animal in the region, and the role the jaguar played in the culture of people who lived there.

Participants were asked to attend a single meeting. The goal of the meeting was to generate ideas about how to engage citizens using the arts in learning about the jaguar. Many ideas were brainstormed at the meeting, and several were put into action. The meeting was so successful that many who came are continuing to work together on additional projects. One group of original participants started a project called Sewing Spots Together. This project involves citizens in creating a quilt that depicts the jaguar. The quilt travels to community events. In addition, a book is being written about jaguars and is being edited by one of the meeting's original participants.[35]

people items with which to fidget. Sweet and salty snacks (e.g. individually wrapped candies and pretzels) keep energy levels up and people at the table.

- **Exploring questions that matter** involves designing powerful open-ended questions that require more than a "yes" or "no" answer. Meaningful questions are thought-provoking and generate energy that can lead to profound results. You may choose to have the café explore a single question or a series of questions that support a logical progression of discovery and requires several rounds of conversation. For example, if two nonprofits were exploring the possibility of partnering on a project, potential questions could include:

  1. What are the benefits of pursuing a partnership on the project?
  2. What strengths does each group bring to the potential partnership?
  3. What would the perfect partnership look like?
  4. At the end of the day, how would we know our partnership has been successful?

- **Encouraging everyone's contribution** is possible by asking all participants to actively engage to make a difference. People support what they help create whether it's through sharing ideas and perspectives, actively listening or both.

- **Connecting diverse perspectives** happens by moving between tables, meeting new people and actively contributing points of view and ideas. This way, discoveries are linked and ever-widening circles of thought are created. This confluence is one of the distinguishing characteristics of the World Café approach.

- **Listening for insights and sharing discoveries** results from practicing shared listening techniques and learning to identify themes and patterns. The outcome is a connection to the larger whole and the emergence of unique insights. After several rounds of discourse, it is helpful to bring the entire group together for a conversation. This offers the opportunity to connect the overall themes or questions that have risen to the top and to capture thoughts for future exploration and planning.[33]

World Café Etiquette

Posting expectations can be helpful to encourage and enhance results:

- Focus on what matters.
- Contribute your thinking.
- Speak your mind and heart.
- Listen to understand.
- Link and connect ideas.
- Listen together for insights and deeper questions.
- Play, doodle, draw, eat.
- Have fun![34]

A copy of the World Café Etiquette can be found on page 209. For a downloadable version go to www.LeadforGood.org.

Open Space Technology

Another tool for encouraging communication and collaboration is Open Space Technology. Developed by Harrison Owen, it is often used in conjunction with World Café. The technology takes themes and ideas and helps groups determine what's worthy of further exploration and possible action planning. Open Space Technology works because self-managed discussion and work groups are allowed to form, leadership is shared, diversity of thought is honored and opportunities emerge to think creatively. The Open Space Technology process has multiple steps.[36] A copy of *"A Brief User's Guide to Open Space Technology"* can be found at http://www.openspaceworld.com/users_guide.htm.

The Take Away

Using strengths-based approaches to build strong community relationships is a key to maintaining a successful nonprofit. Nurturing external partnerships and seeking collaborative opportunities exponentially increases impact. It also ensures sustainability as funders continue to expect resources to be leveraged through interdependent efforts among and between nonprofits and other organizations.

TOOLS ● STEP 6
BUILD STRONG COMMUNITY RELATIONSHIPS

COLLABORABILITY ASSESSMENT

	PLEASE RATE YOURSELF ON THE FOLLOWING ASPECTS OF YOUR COLLABORABILITY	Needs Development				Very Strong
1	Listening skills	1	2	3	4	5
2	Being challenged without taking it personally	1	2	3	4	5
3	Flexibility to accept more than one way of thinking	1	2	3	4	5
4	Curiosity	1	2	3	4	5
5	Openness to different points of view	1	2	3	4	5
6	Willingness to challenge my own thinking	1	2	3	4	5
7	Keeping the goal in mind as I explore an issue	1	2	3	4	5
8	Being able to step back to reflect on my own participation in discussions	1	2	3	4	5
9	Building on other people's ideas without fearing my idea will be diminished	1	2	3	4	5
10	Willingness to speak out about my ideas	1	2	3	4	5
11	Pausing to allow time for reflection and thinking	1	2	3	4	5
12	Asking others questions for clarification or more details	1	2	3	4	5
13	Taking cues from how others respond	1	2	3	4	5
14	Presuming positive intentions of others during discussions	1	2	3	4	5
15	Paraphrasing what I hear to help clarify what is meant	1	2	3	4	5
16	Using the "Yes And" method of accepting another's suggestion and building on it further	1	2	3	4	5
17	Willingness to go with the element of surprise in a conversation	1	2	3	4	5
18	Being able to see failure as a contributor to innovation	1	2	3	4	5

Source: Debra Exner and Maddie Hunter, www.CollaborationPaysOff.com, 2008

CHAPTER SEVEN • STEP 7

ACHIEVE RESULTS

Achieving results requires two distinct areas of focus. The first is ensuring sustainability through fundraising and other methods of revenue generation. Next is identifying appropriate measures that demonstrate impact.

With the changes that have occurred in the economy, nonprofits can no longer depend on one or two sources of funding, such as government contracts or private grants, to keep doors open. Leaders must explore, develop and execute creative solutions. This includes leveraging existing sources of funding to increase support as well as deploying previously untapped opportunities to earn revenue.

> "Effective leadership is not about making speeches or being liked; leadership is defined by results not attributes."
>
> Peter Drucker

Stakeholders, including funders, staff and volunteers, are looking for proof that the work being done is making a difference. They want to know "What" and "How Much" of an impact an organization is having. In other words, the right activities must be measured in the correct manner to prove the programs being offered add value and are worthy of continued support.

Ensuring Sustainability by Diversifying Sources of Funding

For the last several years, available funding from federal, state and local entities has been shrinking and nonprofits have had to find creative new ways to remain sustainable. Even as the economy continues to recover, the new reality is that nonprofits must diversify revenue streams and discover new sources of support. The majority of contributed revenue for most nonprofit organizations comes through gifts from individuals. Nationwide over the last several years, approximately 72 percent of all charitable gifts have come from individuals. More recent data indicate individual giving is on the rise. According to *Giving USA's 2014 Report*, contributions by individuals between 2011 and 2013 represent 73 percent of growth in total giving.[37] With few exceptions, organizations should therefore be focusing their fundraising energies on individual giving through annual campaigns and major gifts.

Common misconceptions abound about fundraising. Many believe that hosting an event is the best way to raise money, or that applying for grants is the gold-standard. Most fund development professionals find events to be among the poorest ways to raise money for a nonprofit. Events require huge investments of time and energy, and can be expensive to hold, even with discounts from vendors or in-kind contributions. For most events, the net proceeds (revenue minus expenses) do not outweigh the expense—and effort—required to put on the event. Of course there are exceptions. Some galas, runs and tournaments attract huge crowds and result in millions of dollars in net revenue.

More typical, however, are events that net $25,000 and take at least a year and abundant staff time to plan and execute. If such an event is coordinated solely by volunteers and/or the purpose is to expose people to the organization's mission thus "friend-raise," then there may be value in pursuing it, even if net proceeds are small. Otherwise, in nearly every case, cost outweighs benefit.

Grant writing, while an important element of diversified fundraising plans, should constitute only one avenue of support an organization pursues. Corporate, foundation, and government grants represent a relatively small percentage of total giving and no organization should limit itself only to that group of donors.

Individual Giving

To effectively generate revenue through individual gifts, an organization must start by being clear on its purpose and message in order to make its case for support. The foundation for this work is to firmly establish the vision and mission of the organization as discussed in Chapter Three. Being able to succinctly articulate your organization's story is critical to successful fundraising efforts. A blank template of the Building a Case Statement for Support Worksheet can be found on page 146. For a downloadable version go to www.LeadforGood.org. It is designed to help you ensure your message is strong and specific.

Identifying Donors

Once you are clear on the case for support, you must identify who to approach with your succinct message. In addition to drawing on your current database of supporters,this is a perfect opportunity for members of your board to get involved by leveraging relationships they have with potential new donors in the community. A core responsibility of a board of directors is to ensure the organization has adequate resources to carry out the agency's vision and mission. This includes fundraising! Executive directors have an obligation to make certain their boards are clear on this responsibility.

Stephanie Small, the founder and former executive director of a nonprofit that provides therapeutic art programs, says, "board members are the primary champions and supporters of all aspects of the organization, including its fundraising. One of the primary responsibilities of an effective board of directors, beyond governance issues, is to ensure continual development efforts. Board members are crucial for building relationships, opening doors and stewarding donors to ensure the organization's viability. They are the most credible representatives of the organization because of their financial and time commitments, their in-depth knowledge of the organization's mission and their willingness to ask for support. Board members are relentless advocates for the organization and are willing to approach their personal and professional networks in service to the organization through financial and in-kind support."[38]

Making the "Ask"

It is the role of board members to identify prospective donors and arrange meetings. The best case scenario is for the board member to accompany the nonprofit representative (whether that is the executive director, development director, or major gifts officer) on face-to-face calls. If the board member knows the prospect well, then it's valuable for the board member to do most of the talking. If the board member is not comfortable making the "ask," her or she can simply be present and show support while the nonprofit representative asks for a contribution. A phone meeting is also an option, but isn't usually as fruitful. A third option is to ask the board member to send personalized letters or handwritten notes to his or her identified list of potential donors asking for support.

Helpful tools for identifying the number and levels of gifts needed and prioritizing potential donors are the Gift Pyramid Worksheet and the Major Gifts Prospect Prioritization Matrix. Completed examples of both of these tools can be found in the Tools Section at the end of this chapter. For blank templates go to pages 177 and 182, respectively. For downloadable versions go to www.LeadforGood.org.

Asking Annually

Annual campaigns are organized efforts to generate operational funding that target current, past, and potential supporters. For many organizations, annual campaigns are a year-round fundraising effort. Others succeed with shorter campaigns, and for them, campaign timing is important. Many such organizations focus on an end-of-year campaign because people are feeling generous during the festive holiday season or are seeking to maximize tax deductions. If your organization is tied to the school year or a particular season, it makes sense to link your campaign to a different calendar.

A well-crafted fundraising letter sent by traditional mail to potential donors is one way to maximize results. In this age of social media, other ideas for an annual campaign include: posting a video story on YouTube; creating a status update for board members to put on Facebook; asking board members to tweet their contacts requesting support; and posting a blog entry on appropriate sites and asking board members to forward it to their networks.

For more fundraising options, refer to Ellen M. Hatfield's chart of Typical Funding Sources & Advantages/Disadvantages of Each.[39] A copy can be found on page 203.
For a downloadable version go to www.LeadforGood.org.

Retaining Donors

Studies show it is far less costly to retain a donor than it is to acquire a new donor. Unfortunately, many nonprofit organizations lose sight of this fact. Fundraising is about building relationships with people, and the most effective fundraisers do a great job of relationship-building with their donors to ensure continued support. While costs associated with maintaining active donors vary widely based on size and mission of the organization, Penelope Burk, author of *Donor-Centered Fundraising,* estimates that it costs

$20 for every $100 given by an existing donor compared to $125 for every $100 garnered from a new donor. According to Burk, donors are looking for three things:

1. Prompt and personalized acknowledgment of their donation.
2. Confirmation that the gift was used as intended.
3. Measurable results of the impact of the contribution.

Burk's research indicates that if donors had these three needs met, then 90 percent of them would give again, with 60 percent increasing their donation the next time they are asked.[40]

Proven methods for effectively communicating with donors promptly and appropriately include:

- Acknowledging large-gift donors (whether financial or in-kind) with a call within 24 hours of receipt of a donation.
- Sending a written acknowledgement within 72 hours to all donors, whether called or not.
- Sending regular newsletters outlining what the organization is doing and how it is serving its constituents (pictures tell more than words.)
- Meeting with the organization's top 20 donors one-on-one for coffee or lunch once or twice a year.

Launching a Social Enterprise

Another key strategy in achieving results and remaining sustainable is to charge fees for providing products and/or services. Such social enterprises have proved a lifesaver for many nonprofit organizations as they weathered economic storms over the last several years. The Social Enterprise Alliance defines social enterprises as "businesses whose primary purpose is to support common good." They use methods and disciplines of business and the power of the marketplace to advance their social, environmental, and human justice agendas.[41]

Three characteristics distinguish a social enterprise from other types of businesses, nonprofits, and government agencies:

DIVERSIFYING REVENUE

An example of a very successful nonprofit social enterprise is the alcohol and drug treatment centers of Gateway Foundation, headquartered in Chicago, Illinois. To address shrinking government funding amid rising treatment costs, in 2005 CEO Michael Darcy began exploring new and different revenue models to ensure long term sustainability. After completing extensive research, leaders identified a gap in services being provided to insured individuals in Illinois needing drug and/or alcohol treatment. As a result, and with strong support from the Board of Directors, the organization made a $10 million investment to establish a new line of business known as the Private Pay Initiative (PPI). The new business is focused on providing drug and alcohol treatment to the self-pay and insured populations residing in Illinois. The goal was to grow the business to $20 million a year in revenue by the end of 2016, with 33 percent of all revenue for the organization coming from non-governmental sources by 2016.

Launched during the height of the recession in 2008, after the first year of operation, the PPI initiative had served more than 300 additional patients and earned $2.5 million in new revenue. The collection rate was a high 88 percent. As of the end of fiscal year 2013, Gateway Foundation had generated more than its $20 million revenue commitment and achieved the goal of 33 percent of its overall revenue coming from non-governmental sources by the end of 2014. To read the case study in its entirety, go to www.LeadforGood.org.

- **It directly addresses an intractable social need and serves the common good,** either through its products and services or through the number of disadvantaged people it employs.
- **Its commercial activity is a strong revenue driver,** whether a significant earned income stream within a nonprofit's revenue portfolio, or a for-profit enterprise.
- **The common good is its primary purpose,** literally "baked into" the organization's DNA, and trumping all others.[42]

In its early days, the social enterprise movement was identified mainly with nonprofits that used business models and strategies to earn income. Today, it also encompasses for-profits whose driving purpose is social. Mission is primary and fundamental; organizational form is a strategic question of what will best advance the social mission. New organizational structures emerging include the B Corporation or "Benefit Corporation" and the L3C Corporation or "Low-Profit Limited Liability Company."

For an enlightening and entertaining book that provides additional information on planning and launching a social enterprise, read *Melons to Money: Growing Food, Lives & Social Enterprise* by Gayle Pincus.

Measuring Results to Demonstrate Impact

Achieving results also means committing to regularly assessing performance in order to prove your organization's value and impact. Having an evaluation-focused culture will enhance organizational effectiveness and improve the delivery of products and services.

A key area to evaluate is programming. Programs are generally the heart of a nonprofit, and it is through their execution that organizations make an impact. One way to get started when assessing programs is to determine whether the programs being offered are the right ones. A recently developed tool described by Jeanne Bell, Jan Masaoka, and Steve Zimmerman, in *Nonprofit Sustainability: Making Strategic Decisions for Financial Viability* provides a framework to determine whether to keep, expand, or eliminate a program.[43] This framework takes into consideration both the impact a program has as well as its financial soundness. While this may sound obvious, many programs continue year after year simply because the organization has always offered it or because there is an emotional attachment to it.

Bell, Masaoka and Zimmerman recommend an organization conduct a financial assessment of each of its programs to determine if it is making money, breaking even, or losing money. After this analysis, each program is ranked as either high or low profitability.

Next, the organization needs to determine its degree of impact. The impact assessment encompasses the following categories:

- Alignment with core mission
- Excellence in execution
- Scale or volume
- Depth
- Filling an important gap
- Leverage
- Community

For each program, the authors suggest picking three to four of the impact categories and ranking each on a scale of 1 to 4; with 1 being "not much impact" and 4 being "exceptional impact." Once analysis is complete, scores from each category are added together and each program is ranked as either high or low impact.[44]

Strategy Implications

	HIGH PROFITABILITY	LOW PROFITABILITY
HIGH IMPACT	Invest in these programs.	Keep but control costs. Too many makes an organization unsustainable.
LOW IMPACT	Increase impact & resist adding more until this happens.	Close down or give it away.

Completing both the financial viability and impact evaluations allows you to create a grid that clearly illustrates implications about your existing programs.[45] For example, a program with high impact and low profitability needs to develop and implement strategies to keep costs under control while simultaneously keeping the program strong. A program with low impact and low profitability would need to be eliminated.

Once the strategy implications are clear, it is important to ensure programs are adequately evaluated on an ongoing basis. Carter McNamera, in *"Basic Guide to Program Evaluation,"*[46] identifies three potential program evaluation approaches: goals-based, process-based, and outcomes-based.

Goals-Based Evaluation

Goals-based evaluation looks at the extent to which a program is meeting predetermined goals or objectives. As described in Chapter Three, Think Strategically, these measurements are often developed as part of the strategic planning process.

Some questions to ask when designing an evaluation to determine if goals have been reached are:

1. How were the program goals established? Was the process effective?
2. What is the status of the program's progress toward achieving the goals?
3. Will the goals be achieved according to the timelines specified in the program implementation or operations plan?
4. If goals are not being met, then why not?
5. What needs to be changed in order to achieve the goals? Should any goals be

added or removed? Why?

6. What are the lessons learned and what changes should be made in the goal-setting process going forward?[47]

Process-Based Evaluation

Process-based evaluation involves understanding how your program works. This type of evaluation is useful if a program is new or has existed for a long period and there are complaints or noticeable inefficiencies that have developed over time. It is also useful for capturing how a program operates for replication elsewhere. Questions to consider when designing a process-based evaluation include:

1. How does the organization determine what products or services are needed?
2. What resources are needed to deliver the products or services and how are staff and volunteers trained to deliver them?
3. What is the process for identifying and/or selecting individuals to be part of the program? And, what process is used to determine what individuals receive?
4. What is the intake process?
5. What is the feedback from recipients about the products and services they receive?
6. What recommendations do staff and recipients have about improving the process or quality of the products or services received?[48]

Outcomes-Based Evaluation

The third type of program evaluation is **outcomes-based**. It determines whether your organization is conducting program activities that bring about results that are beneficial to program participants. Outcomes are usually measured in terms of enhanced learning (knowledge, perceptions/attitudes or skills) or conditions, e.g. increased literacy or self-reliance. The Corporation for National and Community Services offers information about outcomes-based evaluation. Contact the organization through its website at www.nationalserviceresources.gov.

The general steps to accomplish an outcomes-based evaluation include:

1. **Identifying major outcome(s)** to examine. An outcome is the benefit derived as a result of the program or service the organization is providing. Ask, "Why

are we doing this program?" Once you determine the answer, ask "Why is that important?" The answer will generally help you identify the primary outcomes intended.

2. **Prioritizing outcomes** identified and picking the most important to examine.
3. Specifying for each outcome what **observable measures** will best indicate whether the program is achieving its key outcomes. This is often the most challenging and confusing step because it requires focusing on specific activities, not just general concepts about how the organization intends to make a difference.
4. **Specifying a "target" goal** for each outcome. In other words, identify what number or percent of clients you intend to impact.
5. Identifying **information needed** to show these indicators.
6. Deciding how to **gather information** efficiently and realistically.
7. Synthesizing, reporting and clearly **articulating the findings.**[49]

Learning-Based Evaluation

In addition to the three program evaluation options outlined by Carter McNamera, another type of evaluation is **learning-based**.

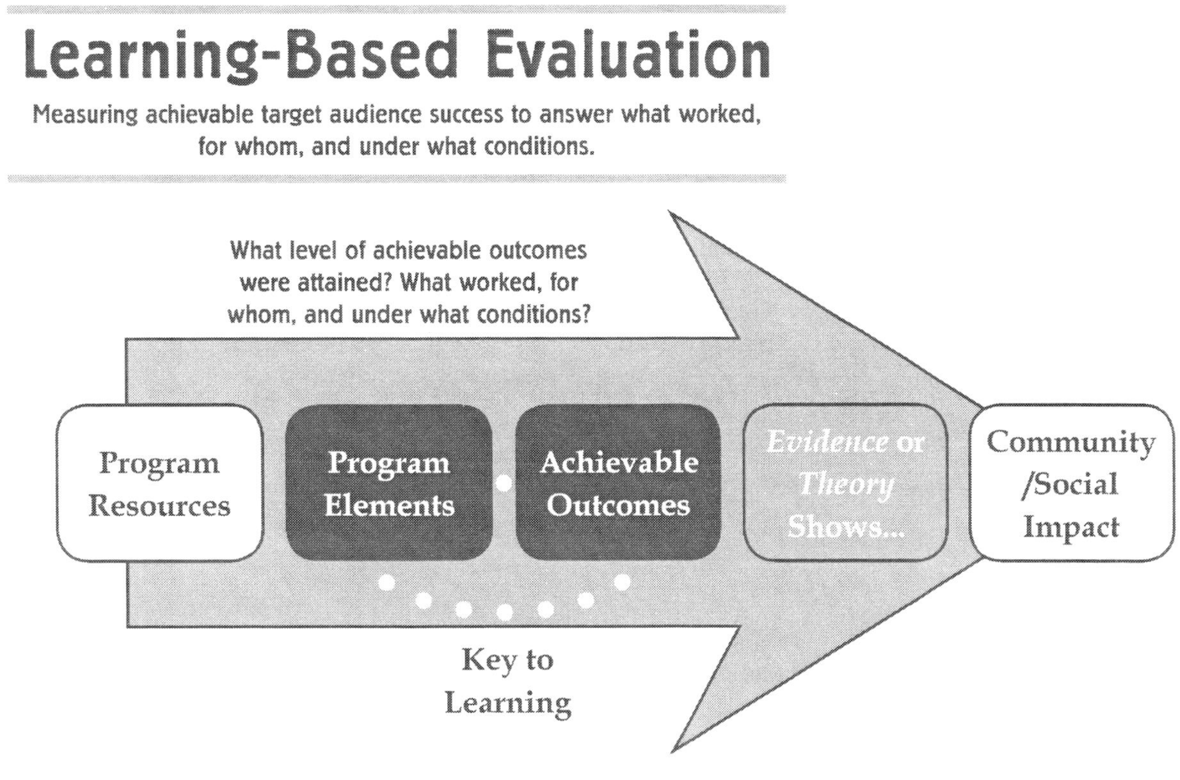

Peter York uses a logic model framework to articulate his learning-based approach.[50] Logic models come in many different shapes and sizes. York's model looks at the resources used in the program, the program components, the outcomes that are considered doable, what the evidence shows, and the anticipated impact.

An example of York's model in action is provided by Literacy Connects. An organization with a strong learning culture, it evaluates its programs and regularly uses the evaluation results to make program improvements and changes. The information is used to communicate with students, staff, board members, funders, and community partners. It helps the organization articulate the "What" and "Why" of its work, share successes, and outline changes it makes to improve outcomes.

What follows are two tables: Learning-Based Logic Model and Measuring Learning-Based Achievable Outcomes.

A blank template of both of these tables can be found on pages 180 and 183, respectively. For downloadable versions go to www.LeadforGood.org.

Literacy Connects Learning-Based Logic Model

PROGRAM RESOURCES	PROGRAM ELEMENTS	ACHIEVABLE OUTCOMES	EVIDENCE OR THEORY SHOWS	COMMUNITY/ SOCIAL IMPACT
Reading coaches/tutors	Program Element 1: Tutoring for struggling readers in K-3 grades	Increase in reading skills; increase in motivation to read; increase in self-confidence; increase in time spent reading	Grade level reading by 3rd grade leads to successful High School graduation, while lack of reading level proficiency in 3rd grade leads to much higher percentage of dropout	Increased high school graduation rate which leads to increases in wages and family well-being
Distribution of books	Program Element 2: Book distribution to children receiving coaching	Increase in number of appropriate and engaging books at home	Number of books in home is correlated with school success. Number of books in home is correlated with less summer decline in low-income children	Increase school achievement which is correlated with earning and well-being
English language teachers/ tutors or immigrants/ refugees	Program Element 3: English instruction for adult English language learners	Increase in proficiency of understanding, speaking, reading and writing English	English proficiency in refugee and immigrant adults is correlated with social networks and reduced social isolation, and increased parent involvement in education which is correlated with children's educational success	Increased family well-being for families and children

Measurement Strategies and Program Outcome Data for Literacy Connects

ACHIEVABLE OUTCOMES	MEASUREMENT STRATEGIES	DATA
Program Element 1: Tutoring for struggling readers in K-3 grades	Student Achievement Test Scores	The program has a statistically significant impact on the DIBELS (standardized test) scores of struggling readers in kindergarten through third grade. The rate of change (improvement) from the beginning of the year to the end of the year was 36% greater for students enrolled in the program compared to those who were not in the program
Program Element 2: Book distribution to children receiving tutoring	Evaluation data collection of books distributed	Students in the program end the school year with 20 books or more in a personal home library. For some students, this is a significant increase if they started the year with no books of their own
Program Element 3: English instruction for adult English language learners	Evaluation data collected through student surveys	97% of students showed increased life skills (primary goal of program) 93% of students showed (primary goal of program) increased self-esteem 58% of students showed increased employment (secondary goal of program)

If You Are New to Measuring Results...

If you are new to the process of measuring results, stick to basics. Joanne Fritz shares advice made by New Philanthropy Capital that suggests:[51]

- **Sticking with what you know.** Don't make measurement harder than it needs to be. Stick to what you are passionate about. Talk about impact in a way that anyone can understand. Don't become abstract and theoretical.

- **Thinking in terms of change.** What does your organization seek to change in its community, people's lives, socio-economic conditions, health-care policy, the environment? Figure out the change you seek to bring, and then how to measure those changes. When you succeed in changing the status-quo, that is an outcome... the outcome you and your supporters want to see. Make sure you capture it.
- **Keeping it simple.** Better to measure just one or two aspects of your program's results, that are at the center of what you do, than try to measure everything. You'll only spread your efforts too thinly and have less to show for it.
- **Asking, "So what?"** Numbers alone don't prove anything. You might provide job training to 5,000 people, but what has that done to improve their lives? What can those people do as a result of what you provided? How many of those clients actually got jobs and improved their lives as a result? Follow your actions to their outcomes.
- **Collecting a variety of data.** Don't focus only on numbers to the exclusion of stories, or the reverse. Value both qualitative and quantitative data. Get feedback from clients and beneficiaries. Collect stories and testimonials.
- **Asking and asking again.** Find out how your services work by asking the people you serve. Ask frequently, using surveys, interviews, and simple questions posed in a variety of settings. Follow up at intervals to measure immediate, mid-term, and long-term effects.
- **Gathering information for at least three audiences.** Measure results while keeping in mind your internal needs (your board, strategic planning needs;) your funders (grant makers and donors;) and your general stakeholders (your users, the public, volunteers, the media.) Collect/measure results that can be used in all of these settings and with all these audiences.
- **Putting adequate systems in place.** When you start measuring and collecting data, you'll need someplace to collect, analyze and store all that information. Set up spreadsheets, get a database, or develop an online system.
- **Treating measurement as an investment.** It will take time, work and funds to measure your outcomes. But it will pay off in so many ways, from increased confidence in your organization to better funding to improved programs for those people who benefit from your work.

In the following table, Carter McNamara provides a brief overview of some of the tools to consider for measuring outcomes.[52]

Selecting the Right Measurement Tool(s)

METHOD	OVERALL PURPOSE	ADVANTAGES	CHALLENGES
Questionnaires, surveys, checklists	When need to quickly and/or easily get lots of information from people in a non - threatening way	• Can complete anonymously • Inexpensive to administer • Easy to compare and analyze • Administer to many people • Can get lots of data • Many sample questionnaires already exist	• Might not get careful feedback • Wording can bias client's responses • Are impersonal • In surveys, may need sampling expert • Doesn't get full story
Interviews	When want to fully understand someone's impressions or experiences, or learn more about their answers to questionnaires	• Get full range and depth of information • Develops relationship with client • Can be flexible with client	• Can take much time • Can be hard to analyze and compare • Can be costly • Interviewer can bias client's responses
Documentation review	When want an impression of how program operates without interrupting the program; based on review of applications, finances, memos, minutes, etc.	• Get comprehensive and historical information • Doesn't interrupt program or client's routine in program • Information already exists • Few biases about information	• Often takes much time and info may be incomplete • Need to be quite clear about what looking for • Not a flexible means to get data; data restricted to what already exists
Observation	To gather accurate information about how a program actually operates, particularly about processes	• View operations of a program as they are actually occurring • Can adapt to events as they occur	• Can be difficult to interpret observed behaviors • Can be complex to categorize observations • Can influence behaviors of program participants • Can be expensive

METHOD	OVERALL PURPOSE	ADVANTAGES	CHALLENGES
Focus groups	Explore a topic in depth through group discussion, e.g. regarding reactions to an experience or suggestion, understanding common complaints, etc.; useful in evaluation and marketing	• Quickly and reliably get common impressions • Can be an efficient way to get a large range and depth of information in a short time • Can convey key information about programs	• Can be hard to analyze responses • Need good facilitator for safety and closure • Difficult to schedule a large number of people
Case studies	To fully understand or depict client's experiences in a program and conduct comprehensive examination through cross-comparison of cases	• Fully depicts client's experience in program input, process and results • Powerful means to portray program to outsiders	• Usually quite time-consuming to collect, organize and describe • Represents depth of information, rather than breadth

A copy of Selecting the Right Measurement Tool(s) can be found on page 197. For a downloadable version go to www.LeadforGood.org.

There are literally hundreds of evaluation instruments available to help you. Go to the Tools, Resources and Assessment for Social Impact (TRASI) for options collected by the Foundation Center at www.trasi.foundationcenter.org. It lists more than 150 resources for measuring and assessing social impact.

The Take Away

Making a difference is the reason nonprofits exist. Key stakeholders, including individual contributors, foundations, governmental organizations, volunteers, and staff are all interested in learning how the work being done by your agency impacts the lives of those who are being served. To ensure your organization is sustainable and able to contribute positively to your community and society, your job as leader is twofold. First, you must guide your organization to be financially sound, and second, you must measure outcomes to prove the work is truly impactful.

TOOLS ● STEP 7
ACHIEVE RESULTS

EXAMPLE
GIFT PYRAMID WORKSHEET

Goal - $300,000

Write your goal in the bottom right hand box in the chart below then work backwards. With your own organization in mind, look over the gift pyramid to identify areas where you are low on prospects, and others where you are better positioned, and modify the chart as appropriate to create a plan to reach your goal that you feel is realistic.

NUMBER OF GIFTS	SIZE OF GIFT	NUMBER OF PROSPECTS NEEDED	PERCENTAGE OF TOTAL GOAL	CUMULATIVE TOTAL
2	$15,000+	4	10%	$30,000
5	$10,000 - $14,999	10	20%	$90,000
10	$5,000 - $9,999	20	25%	$165,000
15	$2,500 - $4,999	30	18%	$220,000
20	$1,000 - $2,499	40	12%	$255,000
25	$500 - $999	50	6%	$273,000
Many	< $500	100+	9%	**$300,000**

Goal

EXAMPLE

MAJOR GIFTS PROSPECT PRIORITIZATION MATRIX

Make a list of the key attributes you believe a prospect should have if she/he going to make a good major gift donor to your organization. Once completed, share your list with your key staff and board. Come to a consensus on what attributes are important. Then, fill in these attributes on the Prospect Prioritization Matrix. Finally, analyze all your potential major gift prospects and rank order them from most likely to least likely to make a major gift/planned gift.

Use a scale of 0-5 to rate how well the prospect under consideration fits each of the criteria. Add a multiplier (x2) if very important.

In this example, Jennifer Stockton, Bill and Sue Michaels, and John Bealton are the best major gift prospects. In these cases, they are connected to the cause or have a linkage to the organization and have the resources to make a contribution.

PROSPECTS UNDER CONSIDERATION	INTEREST or COMMITMENT to ORGANIZATION X2	CAPACITY/ ABILITY to MAKE A GIFT X2	LINKAGE or CONNECTION X2	BELIEF in CAUSE of ORGANIZATION	HISTORY of GIVING to ALL CAUSES	HISTORY of GIVING to RELATED CAUSES	TOTAL
John Bealton	3 x 2 = 6	5 x 2 = 10	4 x 2 = 8	3	5	3	35
Frederica Robertson	5 x 2 = 10	2 x 2 = 4	5 x 2 = 10	5	2	2	33
Bill and Sue Michaels	4 x 2= 8	5 x 2= 10	3 x 2 = 6	4	5	4	37
Ben and Josie Shapiro	3 x 2 = 6	4 x 2 = 8	3 x 2 = 6	4	4	3	31
Jennifer Stockton	4 x 2 = 8	5 x 2 = 10	3 x 2 = 6	5	5	5	39

A FINAL WORD

> Do not go where the path may lead, go instead where there is no path and leave a trail.
>
> Ralph Waldo Emerson

The *Field Guide* has given you seven leadership steps to bolster your success and ensure the sustainability of your organization. Ideas, concepts, recommendations, and tools lie within the pages of the *Guide*. Now it's up to you to decide what resonates and take steps to implement changes into your work.

A word of advice: Prioritize areas you want to tackle so that you are not overwhelmed by the volume of tools at your disposal and not confused by myriad directions you can go. Use the tools provided to create a plan that outlines no more than three activities you intend to undertake over the next 12 months. Let others know you are working on strengthening your leadership skills, including your board chair, and ask for feedback as you experiment and make changes. Determine whether the adjustments are having a positive impact.

Remember, you are not alone. Help is likely available at low or no cost in your community. Once you are clear about your priorities, seek resources that can help you execute your plan. Examples of national organizations available to support you include Social Venture Partners (www.socialventurepartners.org), Service Corps of Retired Executives (www.score.org), Association of Fundraising Professionals (www.afpnet.org), and the International Coach Federation Foundation (www.foundation.coachfederation.org). If these organizations are not available in your community, oftentimes a local community foundation is willing to fund small grant requests to underwrite the cost of hiring a consultant or coach.

As I've chosen my leadership path, I wish you the very best as you pursue yours.

Karen Ramsey
Founder, Lead for Good

REFERENCES

Chapter 1:

1. Tom Rath and Barry Conchie, Strengths Based Leadership (New York: Gallup Press, 2008).
2. Rath and Conchie, Strengths Based Leadership, 9.

Chapter 2:

3. Opportunity Knocks Nonprofit Retention and Vacancy Report 2010 (Georgia: www.OPPORTUNITYKNOCKS.ORG, 2010), 2.
4. Lori Bartczak, "Combatting Burnout in Nonprofit Leaders," Stanford Social Innovation Review Blog, May 21, 2014, http://ssireview.org/blog/entry/combatting_burnout_in_nonprofit_leaders.html, 1-2.
5. Marla Cornelius, Rick Moyers, and Jeanne Bell, Daring to Lead 2011: A National Study of Executive Director Leadership (California: CompassPoint Nonprofit Services and the Meyer Foundation, 2011), 12.

Chapter 3:

6. James C. Collins and Jerry I Porras, "Building Your Company's Vision," (Massachusetts: Harvard Business Review, September 1996), 2.
7. Carter McNamara, editor, "Checklist of Nonprofit Organizational Indicators"(Minnesota: Greater Twin Cities United Way).
8. Peter F. Drucker, The Practice of Management (New York: HarperCollins, 1954).

Chapter 4:

9. Stephen M.R. Covey, The Speed of Trust (New York: Free Press, 2006), 2.
10. Terry L. Cross, Barbara J. Bazron, Karl W. Dennis, and Mareasa R. Issacs, "Towards a Culturally Competent System of Care Volume 1" (Washington, DC: National Technical Assistance Center for Children's Mental Health Georgetown University Child Development Center, 1989), 13.
11. Cross, et al., "Towards a Culturally Competent System of Care Volume 1," 13.
12. Tawara D. Goode, Adapted from Promoting Cultural Competence and Cultural Diversity for Personnel Providing Services and Supports to Children with Special Health Care Needs and Their Families (Washington, DC: National Center for Cultural Competence, Georgetown University Center for Child and Human Development, University Center for Excellence in Developmental Disabilities, Education, Research and Service, 1989 [revised 2009])

13. Peter Salovey and John D. Mayer, "Emotional Intelligence," (New York: Baywood Publishing, 1990), 191-198.
14. Leslie R. Crutchfield and Heather McLeod Grant, Forces For Good The Six Practices of High-Impact Nonprofits, (California: Jossey-Bass, 2008), 53.
15. Adaptation of article entitled "Lobbying and Advocacy – Similarities and Differences" published by Charity Lobbying for the Public Interest, (Connecticut: Connecticut Association of Nonprofits Advocacy/Lobbying Toolkit, 2003), 1.
16. "Advocacy Rules for Nonprofits," (Washington DC: Independent Sector), 1.
17. "Taking the 501h Election," http://www.independentsector.org/501h. Accessed October 13, 2014.
18. Mandy Bass, "Write a Great Talk in 12 Easy Steps," http://freespeakerbureau.com/tips.php. Accessed October 13, 2014.
19. Jim Collins, Good to Great, (New York: Collins, 2001), 22.

Chapter 5:

20. Crutchfield and Grant, Forces For Good, 178.
21. Richard T. Ingram, "Ten Basic Responsibilities of Nonprofit Boards," through NCNB fax network (Washington, DC: BoardSource, 2008).

Chapter 6:

22. Adaptation of article entitled "What is Asset Based Community Development (ABCD)," published on http://www.neighborhoodtransformation.net. Accessed on October 13, 2014, 2.
23. Michael Winer and Karen Ray, Collaboration Handbook Creating, Sustaining, and Enjoying the Journey, (Fieldstone Alliance, 1994), 22.
24. Winer and Ray, Collaboration Handbook, 22.
25. John Kania and Mark Kramer, "Collective Impact," (California: Stanford Social Innovation Review, Winter 2011).
26. Jeff Edmondson, "The Difference between Collaboration and Collective Impact," November 12, 2012, http://www.strivetogether.org/blog/2012/11/the-difference-between-collaboration-and-collective-impact/. Accessed October 13, 2014.
27. Fay Hanleybrown, John Kania, and Mark Kramer, "Channeling Change: Making Collective Impact Work," (California: Stanford Social Innovation Review, January 26, 2012.) Accessed February 29, 2012, 1.
28. Debra Exner and Maddie Hunter, Collaborability Assessment, www.CollaborationPaysOff.com, 2008.
29. Crutchfield and Grant, Forces For Good, 156.
30. For more information about the Philadelphia Multiple Myeloma Networking Group, go to http://philadelphia.myeloma.org.
31. Ada Jo Mann, "An Appreciative Inquiry Model for Building Partnerships," Case Western Reserve University GEM Initiative, http://appreciativeinquiry.case.edu/uploads/PartnershipArticle.pdf. Accessed October 13, 2014, 2.
32. Ada Jo Mann, "An Appreciative Inquiry Model for Building Partnerships,"3-11.
33. "World Café Presents Café to Go," http://www.theworldcafe.com/pdfs/cafetogo.pdf, 2008, 2-4.
34. "World Café Presents Café to Go," http://www.theworldcafe.com/pdfs/cafetogo.pdf, 2008, 3.

35. For more information, contact Cassandra O'Neill, www.wholonomyconsulting.com.
36. Harrison Owen, "A Brief User's Guide to Open Space Technology," http://www.openspace world.com/users_guide.htm. Accessed October 14, 2014.

Chapter 7:

37. Giving USA 2014: The Annual Report on Philanthropy for the Year 2013, a publication of Giving USA Foundation, 2014, researched and written by the Indiana University Lilly Family School of Philanthropy. Available at www.givingUSAreports.org. - See more at: http://www.philanthropy.iupui.edu/news/article/giving-usa-2014#sthash.C4x7xp3g.dpuf
38. Stephanie L. Small, Synergy Partners Consulting, Stephanie@SynergyPartnersConsulting.com
39. Hatfield
40. Penelope Burk, Donor-Centered Fundraising, (Illinois: Cygnus Applied Research, 2003), 31-34.
41. "What's a Social Enterprise?" https://www.se-alliance.org/why#whatsasocialenterprise. Ac cessed October 13, 2014.
42. "What's a Social Enterprise?" https://www.se-alliance.org/why#whatsasocialenterprise. Ac cessed October 13, 2014.
43. Jeanne Bell, Jan Masaoka, and Steve Zimmerman, Nonprofit Sustainability: Making Strategic Decisions for Financial Viability, (California: Jossey-Bass, 2010).
44. Bell, Masaoka, and Zimmerman, Nonprofit Sustainability, 39-51.
45. Bell, Masaoka, and Zimmerman, Nonprofit Sustainability, 55-72.
46. Carter McNamera, "Basic Guide to Program Evaluation," http://www.managementhelp.org/evaluatn/fnl_eval.htm. Posted October 12, 2005.
47. Carter McNamera, "Basic Guide to Program Evaluation,"3.
48. Carter McNamera, "Basic Guide to Program Evaluation,"3-4.
49. Carter McNamera, "Basic Guide to Program Evaluation,"7-8.
50. Peter J. York, "Learning As We Go: Making Evaluation Work For Everyone," http://www.tccgrp.com/pdfs/per_brief_lawg.pdf. Accessed October 15, 2014, 8.
51. Joanne Fritz, "Measuring Your Nonprofit's Results Tips for Measuring Results" http://nonprofit.about.com/od/nonprofitmanagement/a/measuringresults.htm. Accessed October 15, 2014, 1-2.
52. Carter McNamera, "Basic Guide to Program Evaluation,"8-9.

FIELD GUIDE TOOLS

***Register at www.LeadforGood.org to download the following tools. The password to access the tools is:* FG_tools.**

REMEMBER:

***All of the tools listed are available for download after registering at www.LeadforGood.org. The password to access the tools is:* FG_tools.**

ADDRESSING CONFLICT ONE-ON-ONE

- Don't enter into a conversation while angry; consider this an opportunity to improve the work environment, not a gripe session.

- Set up the conversation by saying "I have a difficult situation I need to discuss with you. Is this a good time for us to meet?"

- When preparing for the discussion, be clear on FACTS and don't make assumptions.

- Come from a position of curiosity; ask yourself "Why would a reasonable person do/say this?" and be open to learning why.

- When sharing your concerns or perspective, speak in terms of "I" not "you."

- Pay attention and make eye contact.

- Be respectful and don't interrupt.

- Build on what has been said.

- Focus on issues that are solvable.

- Listen for understanding rather than thinking about your response.

- If you receive constructive feedback, say "thank you."

APPRECIATIVE INTERVIEW/PEAK EXPERIENCE EXERCISE

Think of a time...

If possible, find a partner for this exercise and interview each other using the following questions. Take notes of your partner's responses, as legibly as possible, and return the handout to him/her for later use. Complete questions 1-3 with your partner and then switch roles. Note: While the potential exists to have a meaningful outcome by completing this exercise just by writing down your thoughts in response to each question, it is generally far more powerful to talk through your answers with another person.

1. Think of a time in your life when you felt really energized, engaged and happy at work. This could be during volunteer work or a paid position. Remember a time when you were excited about getting up and heading out to the job and time at work just flew by. What made it such a peak time? Write down your thoughts about the situation, the type of work you were doing and what made it so enjoyable.

2. Without being too humble, what was it about you that made the experience so joyful? Describe in detail these qualities, the strengths you contributed and what you value most about yourself. Also, what was it about the work, the contribution of others and the work environment that enabled you to perform so well?

3. Imagine it is one year from today and you are happy and fulfilled at work. What are you doing and what does this success look like? How are you working differently, and what factors led to the change?

BEHAVIORAL INTERVIEW QUESTION OPTIONS

1. Tell me about a time you achieved something outstanding, a significant accomplishment. What was the situation? What did you do? What was the outcome?

2. Tell me about a recent mistake you've made? What was the situation? What did you do? What was the outcome?

3. Tell me about a difficult customer service interaction. What was the situation? What did you do? What was the outcome?

4. Describe a time when you had a difficult problem to solve. What was the problem? What did you do? What was the outcome?

5. Tell me about the best boss you ever had. What was it that made him/her so great? How did his/her style impact you? What was the result?

6. Describe the worst boss you ever had. What was it that made him/her so bad? How did his/her style impact you? What was the result?

7. Tell me about a time you disagreed with your boss. What was the situation? What did you do? What was the result?

8. Describe a time you had more work to do than you could handle. What was the situation? What did you do about it? What was the outcome?

9. Give an example of how you successfully led a team. What was the situation? What role did you play? What was the result?

10. Tell me about a time you had to terminate an employee. What was the situation? What did you do? What was the outcome?

11. Describe a time you successfully motivated your staff to achieve a goal. What was the situation? What did you do? What was the result?

BOARD OF DIRECTORS APPLICATION

Name ______________________________ Home phone ____________________

Address ____________________________ City ___________ State __ Zip ______

Occupation/Business ____

Work Phone __________________________ Work Fax _______________________

Email ____

What skills, knowledge, education and/or experience could you bring to board of directors?

	Accounting		Management		Community Relations	
	Finance		Fundraising		Human Resources	
	Marketing		Advocacy		Public Speaking	
	Event Planning		Training		Strategic Planning	
	Leadership		Legal		Public Relations	
	Technology		Program/Product		Other:	

What gifts and strengths do you bring to the board?___________________________

____

____

What additional interests, experiences or contacts could you bring to the board of directors?____

____

On what other boards have you served?_____________________________________

____

Do you currently serve on another board? If so, which one(s)? Do you anticipate any conflict?____

In what charitable or community activities have you participated?__________________

____

BOARD OF DIRECTORS APPLICATION - Page 2

Can you regularly attend board meetings on________________? (Please circle.) Yes No

Are you immediately available and willing to serve? (Please circle.) Yes No

Is there any impediment to your attendance at regular board meetings? (Please circle.) Yes No

How much time, on a monthly basis, are you willing to give? ______________________

Will you be willing to make a financial commitment?______________________________

Why are you interested in participating on the board of directors? __________________

____

____

Please supply any other information that you believe should be considered in evaluating your application to be a member of the board of directors:________________

____

____

I understand that my nomination is at the pleasure of the Nominating Committee. I understand that the Nominating Committee seeks persons of the highest personal and professional integrity. I certify that:

- The information supplied in this self-nomination is complete and accurate to the best of my knowledge,
- I understand that if I provided false or misleading information it may be cause for disqualification from consideration in this process and that if it is discovered after I might be selected as a board member, it may be cause for removal from that position,

BOARD OF DIRECTORS APPLICATION - Page 3

- I understand that the information supplied to the Nominating Committee in this process will be maintained as confidential, but I authorize the Nominating Committee and its agents to verify the accuracy of the information I have provided and to use the information I have provided for all purposes related to this nomination process, and

- I understand that further and more detailed responses might be required of me if I become a final candidate.

I hereby give my permission for this nomination.

Signature:____________________________________

Date:___________________________

Nominated by:____________________________________

Please Attach a Resume or Bio

BOARD MEMBER JOB DESCRIPTION

JOB TITLE:________________________ EFFECTIVE DATE:________________________

REPORTS TO:______________________ REVISION DATE:________________________

PURPOSE:

PRINCIPLE ACCOUNTABILITIES:

QUALIFICATIONS:

BOARD RECRUITMENT MATRIX

To use, start by putting the initials of each current board member into the appropriate box, based on his/her attributes. It will give you an indication where you have gaps in order to appropriately recruit new board members. The matrix is set up to accommodate 18 board members who serve three-year terms. The number of columns and number of "classes" should be changed to match the number of board members and term lengths outlined in the organization's by-laws.

	CLASS OF 2018						CLASS OF 2019						CLASS OF 2020					
GROUP:																		
Female																		
Malc																		
20-35																		
36-55																		
Over 55																		
Caucasian																		
African American																		
Latino																		
Native American																		
Asian-American																		
Other:																		

BOARD RECRUITMENT MATRIX - Page 2

	CLASS OF 2018						CLASS OF 2019						CLASS OF 2020					
DEMOGRAPHIC:																		
Inner City																		
Suburban																		
Rural																		
Other:																		
CONSTITUENCY:																		
Business																		
Government																		
Program/Product User																		
Community																		
Other:																		
SKILLS:																		
Fundraising																		
Public Relations																		
Planning																		
Financial																		
Human Resources																		
Legal																		
Program/Product Expertise																		
Technology																		
Other:																		

BUILDING A CASE STATEMENT FOR SUPPORT WORKSHEET

Everyone involved with your organization, whether staff or volunteer, should have a clear understanding of your organization's vision, mission, and strategic direction and should be able to clearly articulate the organization's message to others. These questions serve as a starting point. The answers assist in developing a compelling message and crafting grant requests.

Why do you exist?

Who do you serve?

What do you value?

Why should anyone care? What's the problem you need to address?

How are you making a difference? What's the unique solution your organization offers?

What's in it for the donor? What will it cost?

CHECKLIST OF NONPROFIT ORGANIZATIONAL INDICATORS

How to Use the Tool

The checklist indicators represent what is needed to have a healthy, well-managed organization. Since it is a self-assessment tool, organizations should evaluate themselves honestly against each issue and use the response to change or strengthen its administrative operations.

Ratings:

Each indicator is rated based on its importance to the operation and effectiveness of any nonprofit organization. The ratings are:

E: Indicators with an "E" are essential or basic requirements to the operations of all nonprofit organizations. Organizations that do not meet the requirements of these indicators could place their organizations in jeopardy.

R: An "R" rating signifies these indicators are recommended as standard practice for effective nonprofit organizations.

A: Additional indicators that organizations can implement to enhance and strengthen their management operations and activities are rated with an "A."

Checklist Responses:

Organizations can respond in one of three ways to each indicator used:

1. ***Needs work*** - An indicator is marked as "Needs Work" implies work has been done toward achieving this goal. The organization is aware of the need for this indicator, and is working toward attaining it.
2. ***Met*** - All indicators marked as "Met" demonstrate the organization has fulfilled an essential management need. However, the organization should review these indicators in the future to be sure its management remains healthy in view of the many internal and external changes that occur in all organizations.
3. ***N/A*** - Indicators marked as "N/A" can mean several things, including:
   - The indicator is not applicable to the management operations of this organization.
   - The organization is not sure of the need to meet the requirements of this indicator.
   - The organization has not met, nor is it working on this indicator presently, but may address it in the future.

CHECKLIST OF NONPROFIT ORGANIZATIONAL INDICATORS - Page 2

All organizations should take note: All responses to indicators should be reviewed carefully to see if they could improve management operations. Indicators checked "N/A" due to uncertain applicability to the organization must be further reviewed to determine if they should become a part of "doing business." If the assessors simply do not know what the indicator means, further information may be needed to accurately assess the feasibility of its application. Indicators marked "N/A" because they have not been met but that apply to the organization, may require immediate attention. Technical assistance, consulting, or training may be required to implement these indicators.

The indicators in this checklist should be informative and thought-provoking. The checklist can be used to achieve not only a beginning level of good management, but also improve existing management by providing the organization with greater stability, reliability and success in the nonprofit community. It is also a useful tool if an organization is experiencing management problems, to help pinpoint weaknesses so action can be taken or assistance sought to improve the organization's health. All organizations should use the checklist to re-assess themselves periodically to ensure compliance with established rules and regulations, and to continue improving administrative health through the indicator's helpful suggestions.

RATING	LEGAL INDICATORS	MET	NEEDS WORK	N/A
E	1. All relevant filings to the Secretary of State are current. These filings might include: Annual Registration, Articles of Incorporation with all amendments, Change of Corporate Name, Change of Corporate Address. (The particular state office that processes these filings depends on which state you live in.)			
E	2. The organization is registered with and has filed its annual report with the Attorney General's Office. (The particular state office that processes these filings depends on which state you live in.)			
E	3. The organization has filed the IRS form 1023 (application for 501(c) status, if applicable,) has received a letter of determination, and it is available for public inspection. This requirement applies to tax-exempt organizations.			
E	4. IRS form 990 and 990T (unrelated business income) if required, have been filed and copies of the 990 are available to the public. This requirement applies to tax-exempt organizations.			
E	5. Federal and state payroll tax withholding payments are current. This requirement applies to organizations with employees.			
E	6. Quarterly and annual payroll report filings are current. This requirement applies to organizations with employees.			

RATING	LEGAL INDICATORS	MET	NEEDS WORK	N/A
E	7. The organization has filed with the appropriate State Economic Security agency and complies with all filing requirements of the State's Unemployment Fund. (This requirement varies among states. Contact the Attorney General's or Secretary of State's office for any filing requirements.)			
E	8. If the organization has qualified employee health and retirement benefit plans, they meet all federal laws, including: COBRA; initial IRS registration; plan documents; annual filings of the 5500 C/R with copies available to employees. This requirement applies to organizations with employees.			
E	9. Organization acknowledges and discloses to its board and auditor any lawsuits or pending legislation which may have a significant impact on the organization's finances and/or operating effectiveness.			
E	10. When the Board of directors makes decisions, a quorum is present and minutes are maintained.			
E	11. If the organization is subject to sales tax, state and city filings and payments are current.			
E	12. Organizations that participate in grassroots or direct lobbying have complied with all filings and government regulations.			
E	13. Organizations that conduct charitable gambling have complied with government regulations.			
E	14. Organizations with employees represented by a union must have copies of the union contracts on file.			
E	15. Organizations that operate in a fiscal or host-organization relationship with another organization or social service group have a written agreement on file.			

RATING	GOVERNANCE (BOARD OF DIRECTOR) INDICATORS	MET	NEEDS WORK	N/A
E	1. The roles of the board and the executive director are defined and respected, with the executive director delegated as the manager of the organization's operations and the board focused on policy and planning.			
R	2. The executive director is recruited, selected, and employed by the board of directors. The board provides clearly written expectations and qualifications for the position, as well as reasonable compensation.			
R	3. The board of directors acts as governing trustees of the organization on behalf of the community at large and contributors while carrying out the organization's mission and goals. To fully meet this goal, the board of directors actively participates in the planning process as outlined in the planning sections of this checklist.			
R	4. The board's nominating process ensures the board remains appropriately diverse with respect to gender, ethnicity, culture, economic status, sexual orientation, disabilities, and skills and/or expertise.			
E	5. Board members receive regular training and information about their responsibilities.			
E	6. New board members are oriented to the organization, including the organization's mission, bylaws, policies, and programs, as well as their roles and responsibilities as board members.			
A	7. Board organization is documented with a description of the board and board committee responsibilities.			
A	8. Each board member has a board operations manual.			
E	9. If the organization has any related party transactions between board members or their family, they are disclosed to the board of directors, the Internal Revenue Service and the auditor.			
E	10. The organization has at least the minimum number of members on the board of directors as required by its bylaws or state statute.			
R	11. Bylaws conform to state statute and have been reviewed by legal counsel.			

CHECKLIST OF NONPROFIT ORGANIZATIONAL INDICATORS - Page 6

RATING	GOVERNANCE (BOARD OF DIRECTOR) INDICATORS Continued	MET	NEEDS WORK	N/A
R	12. Bylaws include: a) how and when notices for board meetings are made; b) how members are elected/appointed by the board; c) what the terms of office are for officers/members; d) how board members are rotated; e) how ineffective board members are removed from the board; and f) a stated number or percentage of board members required for quorum to vote on policy decisions.			
R	13. The board of directors reviews the bylaws annually or more often if needed.			
A	14. The board has a process for handling urgent matters between meetings.			
E	15. Board members serve without payment unless the agency has a policy identifying reimbursable out-of-pocket expenses.			
R	16. The organization maintains a conflict-of-interest policy and all board members and executive staff review and sign annually to acknowledge and comply with the policy.			
R	17. The board has an annual calendar of meetings. The board also has an attendance policy such that a quorum of the organization's board meets at least quarterly.			
A	18. Meetings have written agendas and materials relating to significant decisions to be made are given to the board in advance of the meeting.			
A	19. The board has a written policy prohibiting employees and members of employees' immediate families from serving as board chair or treasurer.			
R	20. Board members annually commit to making a meaningful financial contribution, attending board meetings, and participating in organization-related events.			
R	21. Board members complete two annual board assessments. The first pertains to the board as a group, and the second focuses on the performance of the individual board member.			

RATING	FINANCIAL INDICATORS	MET	NEEDS WORK	N/A
E	1. The organization follows accounting practices that conform to accepted standards.			
E	2. The organization has systems in place to provide the appropriate information needed by staff and board to make sound financial decisions and to fulfill Internal Revenue Service requirements.			
R	3. The organization prepares timely financial statements including the Balance Sheet (or Statement of Financial Position) and Statement of Revenue and Expenses (or Statement of Financial Activities) that are clearly presented and useful for the board and staff.			
R	4. The organization prepares financial statements on a budget versus actual and/or comparative basis to achieve a better understanding of its finances.			
E	5. The organization develops an annual comprehensive operating budget that includes costs for all programs, management and fundraising, all sources of funding, and is tied to the strategic plan. This budget is reviewed and approved by the board of directors.			
R	6. The organization monitors unit costs of programs and services through the documentation of staff time and direct expenses and use of a process for allocation of management and general and fundraising expenses.			
E	7. The organization prepares cash flow projections.			
R	8. The organization periodically forecasts year-end revenues and expenses to assist in making sound management decisions throughout the year.			
E	9. The organization reconciles all cash accounts monthly.			
E	10. The organization has a review process to monitor that it is receiving appropriate and accurate financial information whether from a contracted service or internal processing.			
E	11. If the organization has billable contracts or other service income, procedures are established for the periodic billing, follow-up and collection of all accounts, and has documentation that substantiates all billings.			

RATING	FINANCIAL INDICATORS Continued	MET	NEEDS WORK	N/A
E	12. Government contracts, purchase of service agreements and grant agreements are in writing and are reviewed by a staff member of the organization to monitor compliance with all stated conditions.			
E	13. Payroll is prepared following appropriate state and federal regulations and organizational policy.			
E	14. Persons employed on a contract basis meet all federal requirements for this form of employment. W-9s are completed by contractors and disbursement records are kept so 1099's can be issued at year end.			
E	15. Organizations that purchase and sell merchandise take periodic inventories to monitor the inventory against theft, to reconcile general ledger inventory information, and to maintain an adequate inventory level.			
R	16. The organization has a written fiscal policy and procedures manual and follows it.			
E	17. The organization has documented a set of internal controls, including the handling of cash and deposits, approval over spending and disbursements.			
E	18. The organization has a policy identifying authorized check signers and the number of signatures required on checks in excess of specified dollar amounts.			
E	19. All expenses of the organization are approved by a designated person before payment is made.			
R	20. The organization has a written policy related to investments.			
R	21. Capital needs are reviewed at least annually and priorities established based on the strategic plan.			
R	22. The organization has established a contingency plan identifying actions to take in the event of a reduction or loss in funding.			
R	23. The organization has established, or is actively trying to develop, a reserve of funds to cover six months of operating expenses.			
E	24. The organization has suitable insurance coverage, which is periodically reviewed to ensure the appropriate levels and types of coverage are in place.			

RATING	FINANCIAL INDICATORS Continued	MET	NEEDS WORK	N/A
R	25. Employees, board members and volunteers who handle cash and investments are bonded to help assure the safeguarding of assets.			
E	26. The organization files IRS form 990's on a timely basis within prescribed time lines.			
R	27. The organization reviews income annually to determine and report unrelated business income to the IRS.			
R	28. The organization has an annual, independent audit of its financial statements, prepared by a certified public accountant.			
R	29. In addition to the audit, the CPA prepares a management letter containing recommendations for improvements in the financial operations of the organization.			
R	30. The board of directors, or an appropriate committee, is responsible for soliciting bids, interviewing auditors and hiring an auditor for the organization.			
R	31. The board of directors, or an appropriate committee, reviews and approves the audit report and management letter and with staff input and support, and institutes necessary changes.			
E	32. The audit, or an organization-prepared annual report that includes financial statements, is made available to service recipients, volunteers, contributors, funders and other interested parties.			
R	33. Training is made available for board and appropriate staff on relevant accounting topics and all appropriate persons are encouraged to participate in various training opportunities.			

CHECKLIST OF NONPROFIT ORGANIZATIONAL INDICATORS - Page 10

RATING	FUNDRAISING INDICATORS	MET	NEEDS WORK	N/A
E	1. Funds are raised in an ethical manner for activities consistent with the organization's vision, mission and strategic plan.			
E	2. The board of directors and organization staff are knowledgeable about the fundraising process and the roles for fundraising in the organization.			
E	3. The organization's board of directors has established a committee charged with developing, evaluating and reviewing fundraising policies and practices.			
E	4. The committee is actively involved in the fundraising process and works to involve others on the board in these activities.			
R	5. The board of directors, executive director and committee supports and participates in the total fundraising process, including project identification, cultivation, solicitation and recognition.			
R	6. The fundraising program is staffed and funded at a level consistent with fundraising expectations.			
A	7. There is direct communication and a strong relationship between marketing, accounting and other administrative support functions to assist in fundraising.			
E	8. The organization is accountable to donors and other key constituencies and demonstrates its stewardship through regular communications and annual reports.			

CHECKLIST OF NONPROFIT ORGANIZATIONAL INDICATORS - Page 11

RATING	USING AN OUTSIDE FUNDRAISER	MET	NEEDS WORK	N/A
A	1. The organization meets the nonprofit standards of the state charities review council (if one exists in the state, e.g., the Minnesota Charities Review Council provides standards for Minnesota's charitable nonprofits.)			
R	2. If the organization chooses to use outside professional fundraisers, at least three competitive bids are solicited. Each prospective outside fundraiser's background and references are checked.			
E	3. The organization insists on having signed, legally binding, mutually agreed upon agreements with outside professional fundraisers that outline each parties' responsibilities and duties, specifies how the contributed funds will be physically handled, and guarantees the fees to be paid meet the code of ethics outlined by the Association of Fundraising Professionals and are reasonable and fair.			
E	4. The organization has verified that the contracted fundraiser is registered as a professional fundraiser with the Attorney General, as required, and all filings necessary have been made before work commences.			
E	5. The fundraising committee or appropriate representatives from the board of directors review all prospective proposals with outside professional fundraisers and accept all agreements before they are signed.			
R	6. If the outside professional fundraiser plans to contact potential donors directly, the organization reviews the fundraising materials (e.g., public service announcements, print or broadcast advertisements, telemarketing scripts, pledge statements, brochures, letters, etc.) to verify their accuracy and to ensure the public disclosure requirements have been met.			
E	7. The organization properly reports all required information regarding use of outside professional fundraisers, amount of funds raised and the related fundraising expenses as required by state and federal law. The gross amount of funds raised by the contracted fundraiser is reported on the organization's financial statement. The fees and costs of the campaign are reported as an expense.			

RATING	HUMAN RESOURCE MANAGEMENT INDICATORS	MET	NEEDS WORK	N/A
	EMPLOYEES:			
E	1. The organization has a written personnel handbook/policy that is regularly reviewed and updated: a) to describe the recruitment, hiring, termination and standard work rules for all staff; b) to maintain compliance with government regulations including Fair Labor Standards Act, Equal Employment Opportunity Act, Americans with Disabilities Act, Occupational Safety and Health Act, Family and Medical Leave Act, Health Insurance Portability and Accountability Act (HIPAA,) Uniformed Services Employment and Reemployment Rights Act, Form I-9 and E-Verify, Affordable Care Act, and Affirmative Action Plan (if required), etc.			
R	2. The organization follows nondiscriminatory hiring practices.			
R	3. The organization provides a copy of or access to the written personnel policy to all members of the board, the executive director and all staff members. All staff members acknowledge in writing that they have read and have access to the personnel handbook/policies.			
R	4. The organization has job descriptions including qualifications, duties, reporting relationships and essential functions.			
R	5. The organization's board of directors conducts an annual review/evaluation of its executive director in relationship to a previously determined set of expectations.			
R	6. The executive director's salary is set by the board of directors in a reasonable process and is in compliance with the organization's compensation plan.			
R	7. The organization requires employee performance reviews be conducted and documented at least annually.			
A	8. The organization has a compensation plan, and a periodic review of salary ranges and benefits is conducted.			
A	9. The organization has a timely process for filling vacant positions to prevent an interruption of program services or disruption to organization operations.			
A	10. The organization has a process for reviewing and responding to ideas, suggestions, comments and perceptions from all staff members.			

CHECKLIST OF NONPROFIT ORGANIZATIONAL INDICATORS - Page 13

RATING	HUMAN RESOURCE MANAGEMENT INDICATORS Continued	MET	NEEDS WORK	N/A
	EMPLOYEES Continued:			
A	11. The organization provides opportunities for employees' professional development and training with their job skill area and also in such areas as cultural sensitivity and personal development.			
A	12. The organization maintains contemporaneous records documenting staff time in program allocations.			
	VOLUNTEERS:			
E	13. The organization has a clearly defined purpose of the role that volunteers have within the organization.			
E	14. Job descriptions exist for all volunteer positions in the organization.			
R	15. The organization has a well-defined and communicated volunteer management plan that includes a recruitment policy, description of all volunteer jobs, an application and interview process, possible stipend and reimbursement policies, statement of which staff has supervisory responsibilities over what volunteers, and any other volunteer personnel policy information.			
E	16. The organization follows a recruitment policy that does not discriminate, but respects, encourages and represents the diversity of the community.			
E	17. The organization provides appropriate training and orientation to volunteers to assist in the performance of their volunteer activities. Volunteers are offered training with staff in such areas as cultural sensitivity.			
R	18. The organization is respectful of volunteers' abilities and time commitments and has various job duties to meet these needs.			
R	19. The organization does volunteer performance appraisals annually and communicates to the volunteers how well they are doing, or where additional attention is needed. At the same time, volunteers are requested to review and evaluate their involvement in the organization and the people they work with and suggest areas for improvement.			

RATING	HUMAN RESOURCE MANAGEMENT INDICATORS Continued	MET	NEEDS WORK	N/A
	VOLUNTEERS Continued:			
R	20. The organization periodically provides volunteer recognition. Staff continuously demonstrates appreciation of volunteers and their efforts.			
A	21. The organization has a process for reviewing and responding to ideas, suggestions, comments and perceptions from volunteers.			
A	22. The organization provides opportunities for program participants to volunteer.			
A	23. The organization maintains contemporaneous records documenting volunteer time in program allocations. Financial records are maintained for the volunteer time spent on programs and recorded as in-kind contributions.			

RATING	OVERALL ORGANIZATIONAL PLANNING	MET	NEEDS WORK	N/A
E	1. The organization's purpose and activities meet community needs.			
R	2. The organization frequently evaluates, by soliciting community input, whether its mission and activities provide benefit to the community.			
R	3. The organization has a values statement that is reflected in the agency's activities and is communicated by its constituents.			
A	4. The value statement includes standards of ethical behavior and respect for other's interests.			
E	5. The organization has a clear, meaningful written mission statement that reflects its purpose and how it is delivered.			
R	6. The organization has a clear, meaningful written vision statement that reflects what it ultimately strives to accomplish.			

RATING	OVERALL ORGANIZATIONAL PLANNING Continued	MET	NEEDS WORK	N/A
R	7. The board and staff periodically review the mission and vision statements and modify them to reflect changes in the environment.			
E	8. The board and staff develop and adopt a written strategic plan to achieve its mission.			
A	9. Board, staff, service recipients, volunteers, key constituents and general members of the community participate in the planning process.			
E	10. The plan is developed by researching the internal and external environment.			
R	11. The plan identifies changing community needs and leverages its strengths to better serve its constituents.			
R	12. The planning process identifies critical issues facing the organization.			
R	13. The plan identifies 3-5 strategies and creates specific measurable goals that address these critical issues.			
E	14. The plan integrates all the organization's activities around a focused mission.			
E	15. The plan prioritizes strategies and develops tactics, action steps, work steps and identifies process owners and timelines.			
R	16. The plan establishes an evaluation process and performance indicators to measure progress toward achievement of strategies and goals and these results are reviewed regularly in board and staff meetings.			
R	17. Through work plans (which include specific action steps), human and financial resources are allocated through the budgeting process to ensure accomplishment of strategies and goals within the allocated time frame.			
A	18. The plan is communicated to all stakeholders of the organization -- service recipients, board, staff, volunteers and the general community.			

RATING	PROGRAMMING INDICATORS	MET	NEEDS WORK	N/A
E	1. Programs are congruent with the organization's vision, mission and strategic plan.			
A	2. The organization actively informs the public about its programs and services.			
A	3. Clients and potential clients have the opportunity to participate in program development.			
R	4. Sufficient resources are allocated to ensure each program can achieve established goals.			
R	5. Staff has sufficient training and skill level to produce the program.			
A	6. Programs within the organization are integrated to provide complete services to clients.			
R	7. Each program has performance indicators to ensure the program meets its goals.			
R	8. Performance indicators are reviewed annually.			
R	9. The agency collaborates with other organizations to produce the most comprehensive and effective services to clients.			

RATING	MEASUREMENT EFFECTIVENESS INDICATORS	MET	NEEDS WORK	N/A
R	1. Every year, the organization evaluates its activities to determine progress toward strategy and goal accomplishment.			
A	2. Stakeholders are involved in the evaluation process.			
R	3. Evaluation includes a review of organizational programs and systems to ensure they comply with the organization's vision, mission, values, strategies and goals.			
R	4. Results of the evaluation are reflected in the revised plan.			
R	5. Periodically, the organization conducts a comprehensive evaluation of its programs. This evaluation measures program outcomes and impact.			

Source: Adapted from checklist created by Greater Twin Cities United Way and edited by Carter McNamara, MBA, Ph.D.

COACH INTERVIEW GUIDE

Questions to Ask a Prospective Coach:

- What is your coaching experience? (Number of individuals coached, years of experience, types of situations)
- What is your coach-specific training?
- Do you hold an ICF Credential, or are you enrolled in an ICF Accredited Training Program?
- What is your coaching specialty or client areas in which you most often work?
- What specialized skills or experience do you bring to your coaching?
- What is your philosophy about coaching?
- What is your specific process for coaching? (How many sessions are conducted, frequency, etc.)
- Share a coaching success story or two with me. (Request specific examples of individuals who have done well and examples of how the coach added value.)

Source: www.coachfederation.org

COLLABORABILITY ASSESSMENT

PLEASE RATE YOURSELF ON THE FOLLOWING ASPECTS OF YOUR COLLABORABILITY		Needs Development				Very Strong
1	Listening skills	1	2	3	4	5
2	Being challenged without taking it personally	1	2	3	4	5
3	Flexibility to accept more than one way of thinking	1	2	3	4	5
4	Curiosity	1	2	3	4	5
5	Openness to different points of view	1	2	3	4	5
6	Willingness to challenge my own thinking	1	2	3	4	5
7	Keeping the goal in mind as I explore an issue	1	2	3	4	5
8	Being able to step back to reflect on my own participation in discussions	1	2	3	4	5
9	Building on other people's ideas without fearing my idea will be diminished	1	2	3	4	5
10	Willingness to speak out about my ideas	1	2	3	4	5
11	Pausing to allow time for reflection and thinking	1	2	3	4	5
12	Asking others questions for clarification or more details	1	2	3	4	5
13	Taking cues from how others respond	1	2	3	4	5
14	Presuming positive intentions of others during discussions	1	2	3	4	5
15	Paraphrasing what I hear to help clarify what is meant	1	2	3	4	5
16	Using the "Yes And" method of accepting another's suggestion and building on it further	1	2	3	4	5
17	Willingness to go with the element of surprise in a conversation	1	2	3	4	5
18	Being able to see failure as a contributor to innovation	1	2	3	4	5

Source: Debra Exner and Maddie Hunter, www.CollaborationPaysOff.com, 2008

COLLECTIVE IMPACT CONDITIONS REQUIRED

For collective impact to work, meet the following five conditions:

1. Common Agenda: All participants have a shared vision for change including a common understanding of the problem and a joint approach to solving it through agreed upon actions.

2. Shared Measurement: Collecting data and measuring results consistently across all participants ensure the efforts remain aligned and participants hold each other accountable.

3. Mutually Reinforcing Activities: Participant activities must be differentiated while still being coordinated through a mutually reinforcing plan of action.

4. Continuous Communication: Consistent and open communication is needed across the many players to build trust, assure mutual objectives, and create common motivation.

5. Backbone Support: Creating and managing collective impact requires a separate organization(s) with staff and a specific set of skills to serve as the backbone for the entire initiative and coordinate participating organizations and agencies.

Source: Fay Hanleybrown, John Kania & Mark Kramer, "*Channeling Change: Making Collective Impact Work,*" 2012.

CONDUCTING EFFECTIVE ONE-ON-ONE MEETINGS

Setting the Stage

- Set time for meeting in advance (at least 30 minutes) – consider setting up a recurring meeting based on preferred timing.
- Meet in private space and don't allow interruptions.
- If possible, sit at table or side-by-side. Avoid sitting behind desk.
- Prepare observation comments before meeting.
- Start and stop on time.
- Consider this an opportunity to both give and receive feedback.

Possible Components of Meeting Agenda

- What has gone well since last we met?
- What challenges did you face during that time?
- What progress have you made toward your objectives/goals since last meeting?
- What do you plan to work on between now and when we meet again?
- What support do you need from me?

Share

- Positives observed since last meeting.
- Opportunities for learning observed since last meeting.

CONSENT AGENDA ELEMENTS

Minutes of the previous meeting. There is no need to read the text of the minutes of a previous board meeting at a current one.

Confirmation of a decision that has been discussed previously. Some decisions may need a final administrative touch before the board can vote on them. After such details are resolved, the board may vote on the item via consent agenda at the next meeting.

Chief executive's report. To the extent that the chief executive does not have items other than those provided in a written memorandum to the board, the chief executive's report can be assigned to the consent agenda. However, chief executives who prefer to use a few minutes of the board meeting to draw attention to a particular issue outlined in the memorandum should exclude their report from the consent agenda.

Committee reports. Committee reports often contain important information and sometimes recommendations for board approval or resolution. To the extent that such matters do not need discussion and are supported by written materials provided ahead of the board meeting, they may be better assigned to the consent agenda.

Informational materials. To educate members about the organization, staff provides the board with reports and documents that do not require any action. These might include human resource policies, statistics on compensation levels in similar local organizations, a copy of the IRS Form 990 before it is filed, or a real estate analysis of the local market. However, if these materials relate to discussion items, they should be included as a part of that agenda item rather than placed on the consent agenda.

Updated organizational documents. Organizational documents periodically need to be updated. Rather than waste meeting time, updates — such as typographical errors in a document that require board approval, new dates or locations for board meetings, changes to the organization's name or address in legal documents, revisions to the bylaws after changing the title of the chief staff officer — may be added to the consent agenda.

Routine correspondence. The board may need to sign standard letters to donors, renew major vendor contracts (whose terms have already been renegotiated), or confirm a conventional action (such as opening a bank account) that requires board approval as stated in the bylaws.

Source: Adapted from BoardSource

COST OF EMPLOYEE TURNOVER WORKSHEET

HIRING ACTIVITIES	ESTIMATED TIME	COST
Ad in newspaper and/or online	Cost to write & place online and/or newspaper ad	
Application/resume review	___hrs x hourly wage of reviewer	
Set-up interviews	___hrs x hourly wage of scheduler	
Conduct interviews	___hrs x hourly wage of interviewer(s)	
Do background checks		
• Previous employer(s)	___hrs x hourly wage of person conducting checks and/or fee for outside service	
• References	___hrs x hourly wage of person conducting checks and/or fee for outside service	
• Credit history (if applicable)	___hrs x hourly wage of person conducting checks and/or fee for outside service	
• Criminal record	Fee for outside criminal check service	
Conduct new hire orientation		
• Introductions to staff/equipment	___hrs x hourly wage of person(s) conducting orientation plus hourly wage for new hire	
• Fill out new hire paperwork	___hrs x hourly wage of person(s) conducting orientation plus hourly wage for new hire	
• Conduct required job training and policy review	___hrs x hourly wage of person(s) conducting orientation plus hourly wage for new hire	
TOTAL FOR HIRING ACTIVITIES		

COST OF EMPLOYEE TURNOVER WORKSHEET - Page 2

TERMINATION ACTIVITIES	ESTIMATED TIME	COST
Advice for "sticky" situations	Fees for professional counsel, Executive Director (ED) time, and any others involved	
Payout of unused vacation/sick/PTO and/or severance (if applicable)		
Change locks, entry codes, computer passwords, etc.	__hrs x hourly wage of person(s) responsible for computer administration plus fees for locksmith	
Paperwork • Prepare documentation of poor performance or misconduct • Create "off-cycle" paycheck	__hrs x hourly wage of ED and/or others to prepare documentation Fees to create paycheck	
Communicate staffing change • Meet with employee w/witness to fire • Meet with staff to explain	___hrs x hourly wage of ED and/or other leader and employee to do termination ___hrs x hourly wage of ED and ALL ___hrs unproductive time gossiping about event (assume 6 staff members)	
Unemployment payment expenses		
TOTAL FOR TERMINATION ACTIVITIES		

LOST PRODUCTIVITY	ESTIMATED TIME	COST
Overtime paid to staff to cover for work left undone by open position and/or new employee	____overtime hrs x ___hourly wage of person(s) working overtime to get job done	
Wages paid to new employee who is not yet productive	____hrs x hourly wage of new hire while unproductive	
Time spent by other staff members training new employee	____hrs x hourly wage of person(s) conducting training (plus hourly wage for new hire if not included above)	
Unproductive time spent by "lame duck" employee who has given notice	____unproductive hrs x hourly wage of "lame duck"	
Burnout factor for current employees who are sick of having to train new employees and become either unproductive or quit	If enough turnover, may increase absenteeism among remaining employees and/or lose additional employees, etc.	
TOTAL COST OF UNPRODUCTIVE TIME		
TOTAL COST OF TURNOVER		

CULTURAL SELF-ASSESSMENT

This checklist is intended to heighten the awareness and sensitivity of personnel to the importance of cultural and linguistic cultural competence in health, mental health and human service settings. Although it is geared primarily to individuals working in the health field, it has relevance for any individual wanting to assess his or her cultural competence. It is suggested you ignore those questions that do not apply to your work or organization. It provides concrete examples of the kinds of beliefs, attitudes, values and practices, which foster cultural and linguistic competence at the individual or practitioner level. There is no answer key with correct responses. However, if you frequently responded "C", you may not necessarily demonstrate beliefs, attitudes, values and practices that promote cultural and linguistic competence within health and mental health care delivery programs.

Please select A, B, or C for each item listed below:
A = Things I do frequently, or statement applies to me to a great degree
B = Things I do occasionally, or statement applies to me to a moderate degree
C = Things I do rarely or never, or statement applies to me to minimal degree or not at all

PHYSICAL ENVIRONMENT, MATERIALS & RESOURCES

___ 1. I display pictures, posters, artwork and other decor that reflect the cultures and ethnic backgrounds of clients served by my program or agency.

___ 2. I ensure that magazines, brochures, and other printed materials in reception areas are of interest to and reflect the different cultures and languages of individuals and families served by my program or agency.

___ 3. When using videos, films or other media resources for health education, treatment or other interventions, I ensure that they reflect the culture and ethnic backgrounds of individuals and families served by my program or agency.

___ 4. I ensure that printed information disseminated by my agency or program takes into account the average literacy levels of individuals and families receiving services.

COMMUNICATION STYLES

___ 5. When interacting with individuals and families who have limited English proficiency I always keep in mind that:

- limitations in English proficiency are in no way a reflection of their level of intellectual functioning.
- their limited ability to speak the language of the dominant culture has no bearing on their ability to communicate effectively in their language of origin.
- they may neither be literate in their language of origin nor in English.

___ 6. I use bilingual/bicultural or multilingual/multicultural staff, and/or personnel and volunteers who are skilled or certified in the provision of medical interpretation services during treatment, interventions, meetings or other events for individuals and families who need or prefer this level of assistance.

CULTURAL SELF-ASSESSMENT - Page 2

—— 7. For individuals and families who speak languages or dialects other than English, I attempt to learn and use key words so that I am better able to communicate with them during assessment, treatment or other interventions.

—— 8. I attempt to determine any familial colloquialisms used by individuals or families that may impact on assessment, treatment, health promotion and education or other interventions.

—— 9. For those who request or need this service, I ensure that all notices and communiqués to individuals and families are written in their language of origin.

——10. I understand that it may be necessary to use alternatives to written communications for some individuals and families, as word of mouth may be a preferred method of receiving information.

——11. I understand the principles and practices of linguistic competency and:

- apply them within my program or agency.
- advocate for them within my program or agency.

——12. I understand the implications of health literacy within the context of my roles and responsibilities.

——13. I use alternative formats and varied approaches to communicate and share information with individuals and/or their family members who experience disability.

VALUES & ATTITUDES

——14. I avoid imposing values that may conflict or be inconsistent with those of cultures or ethnic groups other than my own.

——15. I screen books, movies, and other media resources for negative cultural, ethnic, or racial stereotypes before sharing them with individuals and families served by my program or agency.

——16. I intervene in an appropriate manner when I observe other staff or clients within my program or agency engaging in behaviors that show cultural insensitivity, racial biases, and prejudice.

——17. I recognize and accept that individuals from culturally diverse backgrounds may desire varying degrees of acculturation into the dominant culture.

——18. I understand and accept that family is defined differently by different cultures (e.g. extended family members, fictive kin, godparents.)

___ 19. I accept and respect that male-female roles may vary significantly among different cultures (e.g. who makes major decisions for the family.)

___ 20. I understand that age and life cycle factors must be considered in interactions with individuals and families (e.g. high value placed on the decision of elders, the role of eldest male or female in families, or roles and expectation of children within the family.)

___ 21. Even though my professional or moral viewpoints may differ, I accept individuals and families as the ultimate decision makers for services and supports impacting their lives.

___ 22. I recognize that the meaning or value of medical treatment and health education may vary greatly among cultures.

___ 23. I accept that religion and other beliefs may influence how individuals and families respond to illnesses, disease, and death.

___ 24. I understand that the perception of health, wellness, and preventive health services have different meanings to different cultural groups.

___ 25. I recognize and understand that beliefs and concepts of emotional well-being vary significantly from culture to culture.

___ 26. I understand that beliefs about mental illness and emotional disability are culturally-based. I accept that responses to these conditions and related treatment/interventions are heavily influenced by culture.

___ 27. I recognize and accept that folk and religious beliefs may influence an individual's or family's reaction and approach to a child born with a disability, or later diagnosed with a disability, genetic disorder, or special health care needs.

___ 28. I understand that grief and bereavement are influenced by culture.

___ 29. I accept and respect that customs and beliefs about food, its value, preparation, and use are different from culture to culture.

___ 30. I seek information from individuals, families or other key community informants that will assist in service adaptation to respond to the needs and preferences of culturally and ethnically diverse groups served by my program or agency.

___ 31. Before visiting or providing services in the home setting, I seek information on acceptable behaviors, courtesies, customs, and expectations that are unique to the culturally diverse groups served by my program or agency.

___ 32. I keep abreast of the major health and mental health concerns and issues for ethnically and racially diverse client populations residing in the geographic locale served by my program or agency.

CULTURAL SELF-ASSESSMENT - Page 4

___33. I am aware of specific health and mental health disparities and their prevalence within the communities served by my program or agency.

___34. I am aware of the socio-economic and environmental risk factors that contribute to health and mental health disparities or other major health problems of culturally and linguistically diverse populations served by my program or agency.

___35. I am well versed in the most current and proven practices, treatments, and interventions for the delivery of health and mental health care to specific racial, ethnic, cultural and linguistic groups within the geographic locale served by my agency or program.

___36. I avail myself to professional development and training to enhance my knowledge and skills in the provision of services and supports to culturally and linguistically diverse groups.

___37. I advocate for the review of my program's or agency's mission statement, goals, policies, and procedures to ensure that they incorporate principles and practices that promote cultural and linguistic competence.

Source: Tawara D. Goode, National Center for Cultural Competence, Georgetown University Center for Child & Human Development, University Center for Excellence in Developmental Disabilities, Education, Research & Service. Adapted from *Promoting Cultural Competence and Cultural Diversity for Personnel Providing Services and Supports to Children with Special Health Care Needs and their Families*, June 1989 (Revised 2009).

DECISION-MAKING FILTER

A helpful tool in deciding whether to add a new initiative is a filter that asks key questions. Creating questions to clarify whether the project is the right fit also helps you avoid mission creep, a phenomenon caused by agreeing to add new programs because money is available, not because the program is aligned with the organization's vision or mission. While each organization needs to decide for itself what questions to ask when considering a new initiative, options include:

- Is this aligned with our vision, mission and values?
- Does it serve our primary customer? If not, does it serve as a relationship builder with an important constituency?
- Does it support a specific strategy?
- Is it a good use of limited resources?
- Is the social or financial impact favorable enough to replace an existing program?

DECISION-MAKING LEVELS OF AUTHORITY

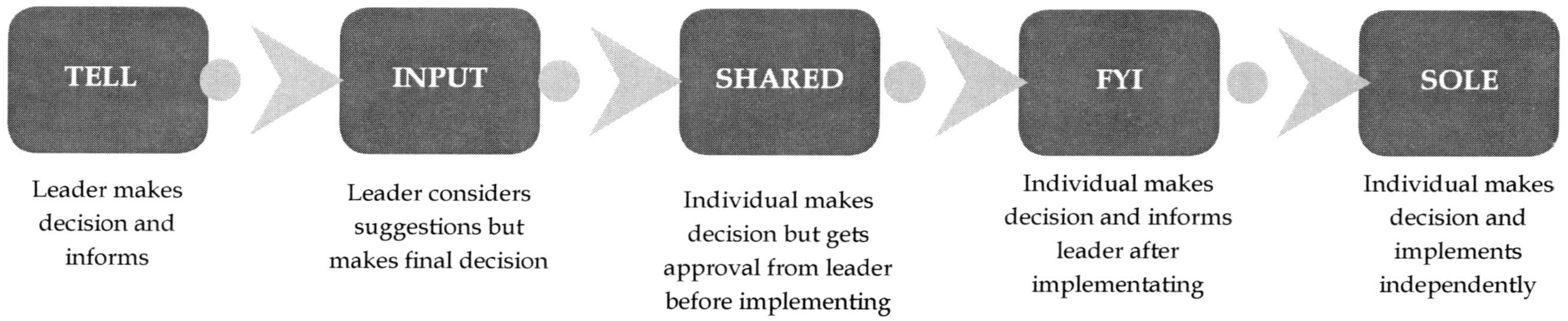

EMPLOYEE JOB DESCRIPTION

JOB TITLE:_______________________ EFFECTIVE DATE:_______________________

EEO CODE:_______________________ REVISION DATE:_______________________

REPORTS TO:_____________________ FSLA:_________________________________

PURPOSE:

PRINCIPLE ACCOUNTABILITIES:

QUALIFICATIONS:

CRITICAL FUNCTIONS:

GIFT PYRAMID WORKSHEET

Goal - $____________

Write your goal in the bottom right hand box in the chart below then work backwards. With your own organization in mind, look over the gift pyramid to identify areas where you are low on prospects, and others where you are better positioned, and modify the chart as appropriate to create a plan to reach your goal that you feel is realistic.

NUMBER OF GIFTS	SIZE OF GIFT	NUMBER OF PROSPECTS NEEDED	PERCENTAGE OF TOTAL GOAL	CUMULATIVE TOTAL
Many				

GROUND RULE OPTIONS FOR MEETINGS

- Start and end on time.
- Be focused and stay on track.
- Provide meaningful content that is relevant to the group.
- Everyone speaks up and interacts.
- Have open and responsive dialogue.
- Respect one another.
- Be honest.
- Be open to change.
- No side conversations.
- Speak up when the meeting environment needs attention.
- Take bio breaks if needed.
- Deliver on assigned action items.

I APPRECIATE

NAME:____________________________________

Because she/he: ____________________________________

And because of that:____________________________________

And because of that:____________________________________

Which resulted in:____________________________________

LEARNING-BASED LOGIC MODEL

Partner with key stakeholders to complete each column. After implementing the program, be sure to review the completed logic model to determine what level of achievable outcomes were obtained. Also identify what elements worked, for whom they worked, and under what conditions they worked. Having this data is helpful for securing funding as well as for future planning.

PROGRAM RESOURCES	PROGRAM ELEMENTS	ACHIEVABLE OUTCOMES	EVIDENCE OR THEORY SHOWS	COMMUNITY/ SOCIAL IMPACT

Source: Peter York

LEGISLATIVE ACTIVITIES ACCEPTABLE FOR NONPROFITS

Acceptable legislative activities for nonprofits include:

- Providing technical assistance or advice to a legislative body or committee in response to a written request.
- Making available nonpartisan analysis, study or research.
- Providing examinations and discussions of broad, social, economic and similar problems.
- Communicating with a legislative body regarding matters that might affect the existence of the organization, its powers and duties, its tax-exempt status, or the deduction of contributions to the organization (the "self-defense" exception.)
- Updating the members of your own organization on the status of legislation, without a call to action.

Source: www.independentsector.org, "*Advocacy Rules for Nonprofits*"

MAJOR GIFTS PROSPECT PRIORITIZATION MATRIX WORKSHEET

Make a list of the key attributes you believe a prospect should have if she/he going to make a good major gift donor to your organization. Once completed, share your list with your key staff and board. Come to a consensus on what attributes are important. Then, fill in these attributes on the Prospect Prioritization Matrix. Finally, analyze all your potential major gift prospects and rank order them from most likely to least likely to make a major gift/planned gift.

Use a scale of 0 - 5 to rate how well the prospect under consideration fits each of the criteria. Add a multiplier (x2) if very important.

PROSPECTS UNDER CONSIDERATION	CRITERION 1	CRITERION 2	CRITERION 3	CRITERION 4	CRITERION 5	CRITERION 6	TOTAL

MEASURING LEARNING-BASED ACHIEVABLE OUTCOMES

Use this tool in conjunction with the Learning-Based Logic Model to record the details of how the achievable outcomes outlined in the logic model will be measured. Determining specific measurements and following through on collecting the data is key to determining the impact of a program.

ACHIEVABLE OUTCOMES	MEASUREMENT STRATEGIES	DATA

Source: Peter York

MEETING PROTOCOL SUGGESTIONS

- Create and send out an agenda, reports and any required reading in advance.
- Set ground rules for behavior while participating in meetings.
- Use a parking lot (a blank piece of paper taped to the wall) to capture unrelated issues that arise during the meeting. Review and address/ assign the items in the parking lot at the end of the meeting in order to stay on track.
- Have minutes with action items include names and dates of commitments.
- Send minutes out within 48 hours after the meeting to give time for people to act on their commitments (if practical and appropriate.)
- For board meetings, create a consent agenda to dispense with wasting time during the meeting reviewing previous minutes and other documents that do not require discussion.

PERFORMANCE REVIEW

Employee Name:____
Review Date:____
Position Title:____
Name of Reviewer:_______________________________________

Accountability Review

Summarize progress on meeting accountabilities during the review period, using employee input. The leader should complete a draft then meet with the employee to agree on the final content.

With Distinction - 1 | Successful - 2 | Needs Improvement - 3

ACCOUNTABILITIES/ JOB DUTIES	ACHIEVEMENTS/ OPPORTUNITIES *(COMPARE ACCOUNTABILITY MEASURE TO ACTUAL PERFORMANCE)*	SELF/LEADER OBSERVATIONS *(USE SPECIFIC EXAMPLES)*	RATING

 OVERALL RATING: ________

PERFORMANCE REVIEW - Page 2

Instructions: Evaluate the performance of the employee based on the accountabilities defined for the position.

What performance strengths has the employee exhibited during the review period? Be sure to note examples of work well done, special projects completed, new responsibilities taken on and/or any other key accomplishments.
What performance weaknesses or difficulties did the employee exhibit during the review period?

PERFORMANCE REVIEW - Page 3

JOB RELATED OBJECTIVES/DEVELOPMENT PLANNING

Indicate below the objectives and development opportunities to be pursued during the next review period and recommendations for meeting them. Be sure to cover performance areas in which the employee needs improvement.

OBJECTIVES	RECOMMENDATIONS

EMPLOYEE COMMENTS

This review has been discussed with me.

Employee 's Signature Date

Reviewer 's Signature Date

PERFORMANCE REVIEW
ACCOUNTABILITY WORKSHEET #1

Name: ____

Accountability 1: ____

Action Steps:

-
-
-
-
-

Accountability 2: ____

Action Steps:

-
-
-
-
-

Accountability 3: ____

Action Steps:

-
-
-
-
-

Accountability 4: ____

Action Steps:

-
-
-
-
-

PERFORMANCE REVIEW
ACCOUNTABILITY WORKSHEET #2

Name: ______________________________

Accountability 1:________________________

Action Steps: **Measurements:**

Accountability 2:________________________

Action Steps: **Measurements:**

Accountability 3:____________________

Action Steps: **Measurements:**

Accountability 4:____________________

Action Steps: **Measurements:**

PERFORMANCE REVIEW
ACCOUNTABILITY WORKFORM

ACCOUNTABILITY	RESULTS EXPECTED	ACTIONS STEPS	STANDARD/ MEASUREMENT	LEVEL OF AUTHORITY	ASSISTANCE REQUIRED
Your three to five major responsibilities. The big ones- the reason the job exists. Action oriented.	**What you hope to accomplish-the reason why you do the accountability.**	**How you hope to achieve the expected results.**	**How you measure each action step.**	**What level of authority is granted to accomplish each action step.**	**From whom do you need help?**

PERSONAL DEVELOPMENT PLAN

List the competencies you intend to focus on over the next 12 months. Pick one area of strength, and one or two areas where you would like to improve. Identify results expected, help you need, and any budget implications.

	RESULTS EXPECTED (Measure Of Success)	TARGET DATE	ASSISTANCE REQUIRED	BUDGET CONSIDERATIONS
Key Competency:				
Action 1:				
Action 2:				
Action 3:				
Key Competency:				
Action 1:				
Action 2:				
Action 3:				
Key Competency:				
Action 1:				
Action 2:				
Action 3:				

PERSONAL VISION STATEMENT EXERCISE

Have a partner read the following instructions and ask each question individually. Take a moment to focus on each question and answer it out loud to your partner before moving on to the next question. Ask your partner to capture your thoughts and musings as you share them.

Instructions: Close your eyes for a moment and imagine yourself as a very old person, wrinkled, slightly stooped, lucid and fully focused sitting in front of a small group of people. As you look out among those sitting there attentively waiting for you to speak, you begin to reflect on your life and describe the contributions you have made to the world.

1. As you look around, what do you see? What are you sitting on? Describe your surroundings.
2. What do you smell? What is the source of the aroma?
3. What are you feeling? Where are your hands placed and what textures do you notice? What are you feeling in your heart and what emotions are at play for you as you tell your life story?
4. Who are the people around you listening to the fabulous recounting of your life?
5. What are you telling the group? Describe the passion that compelled you to move in the direction you chose. How did your passion have an impact? What guided you as you lived your rich and rewarding life?

Now, ask your partner for the notes about your answers. Use this information to craft your own personal vision statement. It should reflect your passion, why you exist, and the contributions you want to make to the world.

POSITION SELECTION GRID

Use a scale of 0 - 5 to rate how well the job candidate under consideration fits each of the criterion. If not sure about a specific criterion, give it a "3." If a criterion is especially important, a multiplier of 2 or 3 may be added.

JOB CANDIDATES	CRITERION 1	CRITERION 2	CRITERION 3	CRITERION 4	CRITERION 5	CRITERION 6	CRITERION 7	TOTAL

PRESENTATION SKILLS CHECKLIST

For each question, mark "S" for satisfactory or "NI" for needs improvement.

	SATISFACTORY (S) OR NEEDS IMPROVEMENT (NI)	COMMENTS
Delivery:		
Eye Contact?		
Volume?		
Use of Pitch?		
Project Energy?		
Posture?		
Meaningful Gestures?		
Rate of Speed?		
Smoothness of Flow?		
Comfort with Use of Notes?		
Comfort with Use of Visuals?		
Introduction:		
Established Bond?		
Aroused Interest?		
Established Credibility?		
Expressed Outcomes?		
Body of Talk:		
Used Concrete Words/Examples?		
Asked Questions?		
Repeated to Make a Point?		
Used Short Striking Statements?		

PRESENTATION SKILLS CHECKLIST - Page 2

	SATISFACTORY (S) OR NEEDS IMPROVEMENT (NI)	COMMENTS
Conclusion:		
Repeated Key Points?		
Summarized?		
Used a Quote?		
Used a Rhetorical Question?		
Brief?		
Strong Emotional Appeal?		
Transitions:		
Between Intro & Body?		
Between Main Points?		
Between Body & Conclusion?		
Visuals:		
Clear?		
Supportive of Presentation?		
Used Smoothly?		
Interesting?		
Overall:		
Well Organized?		
Adequate Supporting Materials?		
Retained Interest?		
Delivered on Expected Outcomes?		

Source: Adapted from R. T. Jacobs, *The Speaker's Primer: A Professional's Guide to Successful Presentations*

QUESTIONS TO CONSIDER ASKING DURING THE DISCOVERY PHASE OF APPRECIATIVE INQUIRY

1. Have you ever been part of a really good partnership? If so, what was the partnership? What made it so good? How did it operate? What were the key learnings?
2. What were the stages of the partnership development? If the partnership were a play with a number of acts, what was the key theme or storyline for each act? What were the challenges and how did you deal with them? What were the key lessons learned?
3. What are your best qualities and skills?
   a. Yourself: Without being too humble, what is it that you value most about yourself as it relates to things you bring to building high quality partnerships?
   b. Your Society or Culture: Every society or culture has its own unique qualities, beliefs, traditions or capabilities that prepare us for building good partnership relations. What things about your culture or society are you most proud of in relation to qualities that might enhance or build good partnerships? Share a story about your culture that illustrates its best partnership qualities.
   c. Your Organization: What, currently, are your organization's best practices, skills, values, methods or traditions that make it ready to be a good partner organization?
4. What is the value of building partnerships with other organizations? What are the benefits and outcomes of forming good partnerships? What are your highest hopes for partnerships?
5. What are the core "life giving" factors in partnerships across organizations, which form a strong partnership?
6. What are your organizational criteria for inviting a partnership relationship with another organization or group? What are the key questions you would ask a new potential partner?
7. In your experience, what are the primary barriers and obstacles to both organizations learning from each other? More importantly, how have those barriers been overcome in your partnership experience? How does your organization approach the teaching/learning process? How do you learn from each other?

Source: Ada Jo Mann, *"An Appreciative Inquiry Model for Building Partnerships"*

SELECTING THE RIGHT MEASUREMENT TOOL(S)

METHOD	OVERALL PURPOSE	ADVANTAGES	CHALLENGES
Questionnaires, surveys, checklists	When need to quickly and/or easily get lots of information from people in a non - threatening way	• Can complete anonymously • Inexpensive to administer • Easy to compare and analyze • Administer to many people • Can get lots of data • Many sample questionnaires already exist	• Might not get careful feedback • Wording can bias client's responses • Are impersonal • In surveys, may need sampling expert • Doesn't get full story
Interviews	When want to fully understand someone's impressions or experiences, or learn more about their answers to questionnaires	• Get full range and depth of information • Develops relationship with client • Can be flexible with client	• Can take much time • Can be hard to analyze and compare • Can be costly • Interviewer can bias client's responses
Documentation review	When want an impression of how program operates without interrupting the program; based on review of applications, finances, memos, minutes, etc.	• Get comprehensive and historical information • Doesn't interrupt program or client's routine in program • Information already exists • Few biases about information	• Often takes much time and info may be incomplete • Need to be quite clear about what looking for • Not a flexible means to get data; data restricted to what already exists
Observation	To gather accurate information about how a program actually operates, particularly about processes	• View operations of a program as they are actually occurring • Can adapt to events as they occur	• Can be difficult to interpret observed behaviors • Can be complex to categorize observations • Can influence behaviors of program participants • Can be expensive

SELECTING THE RIGHT MEASUREMENT TOOL(S) - Page 2

METHOD	OVERALL PURPOSE	ADVANTAGES	CHALLENGES
Focus groups	Explore a topic in depth through group discussion, e.g. regarding reactions to an experience or suggestion, understanding common complaints, etc.; useful in evaluation and marketing	• Quickly and reliably get common impressions • Can be an efficient way to get a large range and depth of information in a short time • Can convey key information about programs	• Can be hard to analyze responses • Need good facilitator for safety and closure • Difficult to schedule a large number of people
Case studies	To fully understand or depict client's experiences in a program and conduct comprehensive examination through cross-comparison of cases	• Fully depicts client's experience in program input, process and results • Powerful means to portray program to outsiders	• Usually quite time-consuming to collect, organize and describe • Represents depth of information, rather than breadth

Source: Carter McNamara, Authenticity Consulting, LLC.

SERVICE ISSUES LOG

Maintain a list of concerns and/or complaints received from external customers. Use it to ensure issues are resolved and to identify trends. Regularly review the log at leadership meetings.

DATE	NAME/ ORGANIZATION OF PERSON WITH ISSUE	ISSUE DESCRIPTION	ISSUE ASSIGNED TO	WHEN & HOW ISSUE RESOLVED

STOP, CHALLENGE, FOCUS TOOL FOR LEADERS

Sometimes, it is difficult to deal with an employee, board member, donor or client who is unhappy or complaining. To keep your cool, and prevent the situation from escalating out of control, the following technique may be helpful:

Stop - Take a deep breath and stop yourself from taking the tongue-lashing personally and keep yourself from responding in the same tone as the person sharing his/her concerns. It's almost never about you, it's about an experience the person has had that was unsatisfactory. Often, she/he doesn't understand the inner-workings of your organization; all she/he cares about is getting the situation resolved.

Challenge - Challenge yourself to really hear what the person is saying. By repeating back to her/him a summary of what you've been told, she/he knows you have heard him/her and the person is much more likely to ratchet back the anger level and speak in a calmer tone. Even if she/he doesn't, challenge yourself to stay calm and professional.

Focus - Focus on turning this negative situation into a marvel of great leadership by giving a genuine apology, if one is warranted, and taking steps to correct the situation. The time to WOW people is when there is an issue or snafu that is handled graciously and professionally. Please don't pass the issue on to someone else in the organization to resolve. Remember, the buck stops with you.

TELEPHONE INTERVIEW SCREENING QUESTION OPTIONS

Name: ______________________________________ Phone: ____________________

Date: _______________

Begin the conversation by thanking the candidate for responding to the posting and asking if it's a good time to be calling. If not, schedule a better time (approx. 20 minutes) for the candidate. Tell the person a little about the job, office location, environment and benefits before asking the questions below. Ask the person if he/she would like to proceed with the phone interview based on the information you've shared. Be sure to take notes for future reference. This intro should only take a few minutes.

1. Tell me a little about your background. What experience do you have working in a nonprofit environment? ____

   ____

   ____

2. What hours would you prefer to work? Are you willing to work additional and/or odd hours if the need arises? Please share with me a recent example when you demonstrated your work schedule flexibility. ______________________________

   ____

   ____

3. If we were to hire you, what date would you be available to start work? ___________

   ____

4. Please describe a difficult customer service or volunteer experience you've had. What was the situation? How did you handle it? What was the outcome?

   ____

   ____

   ____

5. What salary do you expect? $__________________

6. What questions may I answer for you?

TEN BASIC RESPONSIBILITES OF NONPROFIT BOARDS

1. Determine the organization's mission and purpose.
2. Select the Chief Executive.
3. Support the Chief Executive and assess his or her performance.
4. Ensure effective organizational planning.
5. Ensure adequate resources.
6. Manage resources effectively.
7. Determine, monitor, and strengthen the organization's program and services.
8. Enhance the organization's public image.
9. Ensure legal and ethical behavior and maintain accountability.
10. Recruit and orient new board members and assess board performance.

Source: Richard T. Ingram, *"Ten Basic Responsibilities of Nonprofit Boards,"* BoardSource

TYPICAL FUNDING SOURCES & ADVANTAGES/DISADVANTAGES OF EACH

SOURCE	ADVANTAGES	DISADVANTAGES
Individuals	• Largest source of giving • Ongoing source one can build • Once a giver, also an advocate • Volunteers are a good source of money	• Costly to develop, small return per individual unit • Hard to generate unless broad-based direct service appeal • Risky for the inexperienced • Need significant assistance from the organization's board and volunteers
Large-Family Foundations	• Source of large sums of money • Accessible, professional staff • Clear guidelines, process • Most likely to research your request • Board volunteers can help, not always key	• Often only offer start-up funds • Lengthy process • More difficult to access through personal influence • Proposals may be more lengthy
Community Foundations	• Much like large-family foundations • Staff may be sufficient	• Host of foundations within foundations • Most money is earmarked, special funds
Small-Family Foundations	• May fund ongoing operating expenses • Personal influence with board members helps • Guidelines often broad • Not very fussy about grant format	• Hard to access, no professional staff • Often not large sums of money • Without personal influence, may not be possible
Large Corporations / Corporate Foundations	• Can be source of large sums of money • Smaller amounts of money may be ongoing • Often accessible, professional staff • May be tied to volunteer involvement • Business strategy may be clear • Source of cause-related marketing	• Large sums of money aren't ongoing • Hard to get around staff • Must be within their guidelines • Not likely to contribute if not headquartered locally or have a public consumer base • Often want board representation
Small Corporations	• Very informal approach • Money may be ongoing • Personal connections will suffice • Neighborhood focus will help	• Small amounts of money • Narrow range of interest • Personal contacts are key

TYPICAL FUNDING SOURCES & ADVANTAGES/DISADVANTAGES OF EACH - Page 2

SOURCE	ADVANTAGES	DISADVANTAGES
Federated Funds (United Ways, United Arts, Combined Health Appeal)	• Steady source of relatively large sums of money • Clear process • Professional staff, can be agency staff driven	• Generally can't be a start-up organization • Must be social service and fit priority focus • Very lengthy entry process • Very time consuming as must be part of yearly fund raising process, with periodic in-depth review
Government	• Large sums of money possible • Process is set, clear • Political clout helps • May be source of ongoing money	• Application procedures may be long, tedious • May only pay by unit of service, fluctuates • Unspent monies may be returned • Difficult record keeping
Churches and Organizations	• Often looking for group projects	• In-kind services most likely • Need to fit their service focus, neighborhood or religious outlook

Source: Adapted from Ellen M. Hatfield of the Twin Cities in Minnesota

VOLUNTEER APPLICATION

Name: ______________________ Title: ______________________

Business: ____

Business Address: __________________ City: ______________ Zip: ______

Business Phone: __________________ Fax: ______________________

Home Address: __________________ City: ______________ Zip: ______

Home Phone: __________________ Email address: ______________

Cell Phone: __________________ Alt. Phone: ______________

Preferred Mailing Address: ☐ Home ☐ Business

My previous experience with nonprofit organizations includes (list volunteer work, board service, memberships): ______________________________

____

____

My personal involvement or interest in this organization includes (list events attended/ supported, subscriptions, studies, work in the area, etc.): ______________

____

____

I am available: ☐ 8am-5pm Weekdays ☐ Noon Hours

☐ Late Afternoon/Evenings ☐ Weekends

VOLUNTEER APPLICATION - Page 2

Educational Background:

School _____________________ Major _____________________

School _____________________ Major _____________________

How did you learn about volunteer opportunities available at our organization?

____

____

____

My areas of expertise include (check all that apply):

Financial	
	Accounting systems / procedures
	Budgeting and cash flow management
	Financial analysis / planning
Legal	
	Contract review/issues
	Human resource issues
	Real estate
	Articles of incorporation / bylaws review
Development / Fundraising	
	Development plans
	Special events planning
	Proposal design
	Grantwriting
	Public speaking

Organizational Development	
	Strategic planning
	Retreat / meeting facilitation
	Board development
	Program development
	Conflict resolution/mediation

VOLUNTEER APPLICATION - Page 3

	Management / Administration
	Operations/office procedures and manual evaluation/development
	Word processing: ________________
	Work efficiency assessment
	Personnel policies and procedures, employee benefits
	Marketing / Public Relations
	Market research
	Surveys / analysis
	Marketing plans
	Media campaign development
	Collateral development / graphic design
	Focus groups
	Advocacy

	Computers/Information Systems
	Hardware needs assessment
	Software needs assessment
	Hardware/software installation
	Software training/troubleshooting
	Software customization
	Data base management
	Website development
	Systems planning/design
	Other:

I certify that:

- The information supplied is complete and accurate to the best of my knowledge,
- I understand that if I provided false or misleading information it may be cause for disqualification from consideration in this process, and
- I understand that the information supplied is confidential, but I authorize its verification.

Signature:____

Date:______________________________

Please Attach a Resume or Bio

WHEEL OF LIFE

On a scale of 0 to 10, rank how you are performing in each of the areas. Zero is at the center and 10 is at the outer edge of the circle. The higher the number, the better you are doing. If there are areas of the wheel that have low numbers and are out of balance, then take steps to address those areas. Tackle just a few at a time. The wheel didn't go out of alignment overnight, so regaining balance won't happen overnight. Use the Personal Development Plan to outline specific actions you plan to take over the next 12 months. Look at the wheel again in one year's time to see how you are doing and tackle other issues that are still out of alignment.

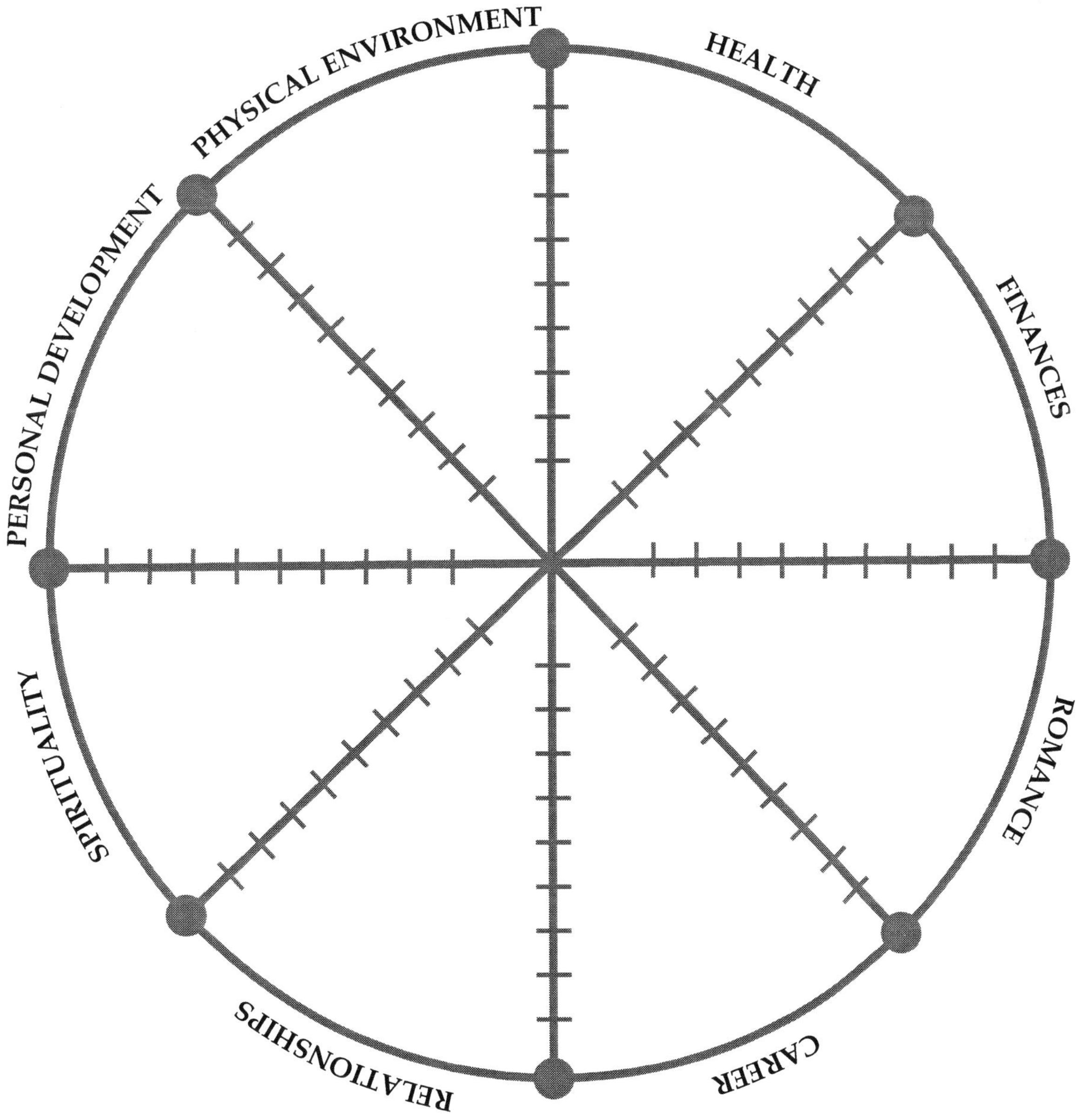

WORLD CAFÉ ETIQUETTE

Posting expectations can be helpful to encourage and enhance results:

- Focus on what matters
- Contribute your thinking
- Speak your mind and heart
- Listen to understand
- Link and connect ideas
- Listen together for insights and deeper questions
- Play, doodle, draw, eat
- Have fun!

Source: http://www.theworldcafe.com

WRITE A GREAT TALK IN 12 EASY STEPS

The easiest and most effortless way I know to develop a great presentation is outlined in these simple twelve steps. By following the step-by-step sequence (without jumping ahead) you will naturally create a successful presentation quickly and easily.

As you work through these steps, other issues, questions and things you need to do in preparation for your talk will probably pop into your head (such as I need to write a bio, what will the set up be?, do they have a screen or a microphone?) It's a good idea to have a separate sheet to jot down and capture these thoughts so you can address them later.

Step #1: Know your outcome

Before you begin developing any presentation, answer the following questions:

1. What do you want to have happen as a result of your talk? (Consider information you want them to know, feelings you want them to feel, actions you want them to take.)
2. What is the next step that you want them to take? Therefore, what type of call to action and/or follow up will you do?
3. How do you want to be perceived by the audience?
4. Considering the above answers, is there anything you need to create, such as an evaluation or response sheet? How will you capture their contact information? Do you want to have door prizes, etc. (DO NOT begin developing the above now–simply to capture your thoughts to serve as a reminder for what you will need.)

Step #2: Know your audience

Often attendees at networking groups are there to see their friends, enjoy a meal and make contacts. It's important that you be clear and honest with yourself about to whom you will be speaking and what they are expecting. Your talk will get a lot more attention if it addresses specific needs and concerns.

Describe your audience:

1. What is important to them about this event?
2. What are some issues your audience really cares about? List interests, desires and concerns. Be specific.

3. How do you fit into the overall schedule? If people are eating lunch while you are talking, for example, it's unlikely that they will be comfortably able to write things down - that may affect what handouts you distribute. Also it means that in a traditional setting some people will have their backs to you. If you are following another speaker, you may want to make sure that the audience stretches - preferably organize a break before you get introduced.

Step #3: Make the connection

1. How will the people in your audience directly benefit from your talk? Example - learn about investing, know how much money they will need for retirement, see what benefits they currently have and where the gaps are, look good, feel better about themselves, make more money, feel more confident about themselves, etc.. Note: there needs to be some direct benefit from the talk itself - regardless if they take the next step
2. Do the benefits above address the areas of interest and concern for the members of your audience? How?

Step #4: Clarify your win-win outcome

How does your presentation benefit both you and the audience?

Step #5: Define Criteria

List parameters and criteria you want to work within. (e.g. length of talk, number of attendees, audio visual requirements or limitations, room set-up, will you be speaking while people are eating/drinking, will alcohol be served, and the time of the presentation.)

Step #6: Brainstorm your ideas

If time, money and energy were not a consideration, what would you say about your topic? Generate ideas in a random, non-linear fashion. Use 3x5 cards and write each idea on a separate card. This will save you time in the organizational phase of this project. Don't judge or make decisions in this step, rather get all your ideas out no matter how ridiculous they seem!

Step #7: Organize your ideas

1. Group your points together by using color highlighters or pencils. If you prefer, you can organize your points in a linear fashion with headings and sub-headings.
2. Now rewrite your main points in order of priority.
3. Identify 1 - 4 major ideas (no more than one major idea per ten minutes.)
4. Under each major idea collect:
   - Supporting facts
   - Stories or case histories
   - Examples demonstrating the idea
   - Research
   - Statistics
   - Other relevant information
5. Make sure the talk:
   - Grabs attention
   - Stimulates interest
   - Builds desire to know more
   - Moves the audience to action

Step #8: Write the body of the talk

Leave the opening and close to last. They require the most attention and you want to make sure you are satisfied with the content before you begin and end your talk. After organizing your data in step 7, you should have a general outline of the main points of your talk. Here are some tips for keeping your audience interested:

1. As you develop the content, keep in mind that people make emotional decisions, which they justify with reason.
2. Keep your talk balanced with soft issues and factual information.
3. If you really want to make a point, you must say the same thing several times in a variety of ways.
4. Stories and examples are excellent ways of demonstrating your point and creating an emotional response.
5. Use facts and data to accent your points. Facts can help you prove your point; they can also lose your audience.

6. Use a variety of any of the following patterns:
   - Story – point – data – story
   - Point – data – story – point
   - Data – point – story – story – point
   - Point – story – data – story
   - Story – point – story – data
   - Data – story – point
7. Be sure to communicate each point's benefit to the audience.
8. You may find it easier to work on the transitions between points after the rest of the talk is completed.
9. Many people like to write their whole talk out. If you do this, make sure you crunch it into an outline. Do not "read" your talk. (I usually write out key phrases and transitions between points. I find it valuable to spend time on the transitions so the talk seems smooth even if I am speaking extemporaneously on the main points.)
10. It's important to practice your stories. Eliminate unnecessary elements and focus only on the relevant details. This will allow your audience to better visualize your stories.
11. 100 words on paper equals about one spoken minute.
12. When preparing a long talk, use fifteen minute modules to keep you on track.
13. Ruthlessly edit your talk. The shorter and more succinct it is, the more your audience will appreciate you.

Step #9: Write a pre-body

Write an enticing "ad" that summarizes the main points and benefits of the body of your talk. You will use your pre-body to help you transition between the opening and the body of your talk.

Example: "Today I am going to share with you the four keys to doubling your income. You will discover how you can naturally and easily increase your productivity by reducing your stress levels; stay focused, positive and motivated; become more creative in your ability to solve problems and, more importantly, overcome limiting belief systems that are preventing you from being your very best... And you can do all this by simply changing the way you think about things. I will show you how!"

Step #10: Visual aids & handouts

1. What points in your talk could be understood more easily with visual aids?
2. Do you want to make a PowerPoint presentation? Keep in mind that PowerPoint can help you stay on track and provide an outline for your talk. However, it can also distract and disconnect you from your audience. Make sure you are comfortable with using your equipment before you do your talk.
3. Keep in mind, words slides require white space. Limit each slide to no more than seven words across and five lines down.
4. If you choose PowerPoint, what style would lend itself to your specific presentation? Consider cartoons, photographs, illustrations, key points without graphics, etc.
5. Are there props or other physical demonstrations that can make your point in an entertaining way?
6. If you use PowerPoint, you can make copies and use them for handouts.
7. Fill-in-the-blank handouts are great for involving the audience.
8. Make sure that your audience has something with your name and contact information so that they get in touch with you later.
9. A program evaluation form is an excellent way to get follow-up information from your audience. The feedback they give you will be invaluable in improving your presentation for the future.

Step #11: Plan the opening

1. Plan your greeting. If you are being introduced, thank the person who introduced you, greet the audience and then pause a few seconds before you begin.
2. There are six effective ways to open your presentation:
   - Tell a personal story.
   - Arouse suspense by asking a question or beginning a story that you don't answer or finish until the end of the presentation.
   - State a fact that will grab their attention. For it to be effective, say it with emphasis and then pause for a few seconds.
   - Ask a question and request a show of hands. Raise your own hand and be ready to back up your question with another if no one raises his or her hand. Example: "How many of you have been to Oklahoma?" If no response, then ask "How many of you like to travel?"

- Promise to give them something they can use.
- Surprise them with a prop that relates to your topic.

3. Do NOT start off by telling a joke or making apologies. If you do have to apologize for something, be brief, matter-of-fact and turn it into something positive.

Step #12: Create the close

1. How you close your presentation is very important. What do you want your audience to do or think about when you leave the stage?
2. If you are going to take questions, ASK FOR THEM BEFORE YOU CLOSE ("Before I close, are there any questions?")
3. It's best to end your talk on a high note by:
   - A strong call for action (e.g. "Do you see how easy it is to create an effective presentation? So if you want to position yourself as an authority in front of a whole room of qualified prospects, I urge you to get started today. Just take it one step at a time. Begin by deciding what you want. Take the first step now!")
   - A summary followed by a benefit (e.g., "To review what we have discussed… and if you follow these twelve steps you will quickly and easily create a presentation your audience will LOVE!")
   - A memorized quotation. Be sure to credit the author.
   - Ending the mystery story you told at the beginning of the talk.
   - Telling a story. For example, "I remember berating myself after my first presentation. I thought about all the things I could have, should have done... but over the years, at least five people who attended that presentation have sought me out and told me that my talk changed their lives. And that's what you will do when you get out there and start speaking. You have the power to change people's lives. And you will."

Source: Adapted from Mandy Bass, *"How to Write a Great Talk in 12 Easy Steps"*

The cover and interior of this *Field Guide*
designed by Amanda Graff
dreamgraffx.com